TEN POPES WHO SHOOK THE WORLD

TEN POPES
WHO SHOOK
THE WORLD

EAMON DUFFY

YALE UNIVERSITY PRESS
NEW HAVEN AND LONDON

Copyright © 2011 Eamon Duffy
By arrangement with the BBC
The BBC logo is a trade mark of the British Broadcasting Corporation and is used under licence
BBC logo © BBC 1996

10 9 8 7 6 5 4 3 2 1

Printed in the UK by TJ International

Library of Congress Cataloging-in-Publication Data
Duffy, Eamon.
  Ten popes who shook the world / Eamon Duffy.
      p. cm.
  Includes index.
  ISBN 978-0-300-17688-9 (alk. paper)
  1. Papacy--History. 2. Papacy--Biography.
3. Catholic Church--History. 4. Church history. I. Title.
  BX955.3.D84 2011
  282.092'2--dc23
  [B]

                          2011029717

CONTENTS

LIST OF ILLUSTRATIONS

Veduta della Basilica e Piazza di S. Pietro in Vaticano

The pink granite Egyptian obelisk erected in AD 37 in the Vatican circus by Caligula was moved to its present position in the centre of St Peter's Square by Pope Sixtus V in 1586. It was traditionally believed to be the last object seen by the dying St Peter.

INTRODUCTION

The papacy is an institution that matters, whether or not one is a religious believer. The succession of the popes, all 262 of them, is the world's most ancient dynasty. The Roman Empire was young when the popes first emerged onto the stage of history, and the earliest references to them, in the late second century, already claim for the bishop of Rome a status greater than that of any other Christian leader. Eighteen centuries on, the popes exercise a quasi-monarchic rule over the world's largest religious organisation. They touch the consciences, or at any rate the opinions, of almost a fifth of the human race. The papacy has endured and flourished under emperors, kings and robber barons, under republican senates and colonial occupations, in confrontation or collaboration with demagogues and democrats. And by hook or by crook, it has survived them all.

How does one represent in the space of ten short chapters a history that straddles two thousand years and includes a succession of more than 260 office-holders? How does one sum up an institution whose mindset and structures derive more or less equally from the sacred books of ancient Israel and the law codes of ancient Rome, yet which has evolved into one of the world's most successful global corporations? Does papal history follow its own distinctive rhythms, or are the popes best understood as players in world politics and chronicled therefore in relation to the rise and fall of secular dynasties, the waxing and waning of empires or political revolutions? Is the history of the popes the institutional unfolding of a single set of ideas, or a chronicle of happenstance, opportunism and serendipity? Is the papacy a coherent project, or an historical conglomerate whose only consistency lies in its protean capacity for survival by adaptation?

The popes themselves have never been in doubt about the coherence of papal history, or its source. From the beginning they have claimed divine warrant for their office as an institution established by Christ himself, destined to endure as long as the human race. In the key papal text from St Matthew's Gospel, the papacy (in the person of St Peter) is described as the rock on which the Church is founded, 'and the gates of hell shall not prevail against it'.

Historians, whether or not they concede the religious claim, have been inclined to agree about the institutional consistency. The great Cambridge medievalist Walter Ullmann, arguably the most influential papal historian of recent times, found it in a single guiding idea. He argued that by the end of the fourth century the papacy had already evolved a mature understanding of itself as the sole source of order and authentic teaching for the whole Christian Church. Over the next millennium, he opined, the story of the popes, and indeed of Europe, was the struggle to embody that exalted self-understanding in a universal code of law and the theocratic organisation of society under papal government. For Ullmann that struggle manifested itself above all in the contentions between popes and emperors, in which the popes of the high Middle Ages were (for a time) the victors, able and willing both to shake and to settle the world and its kingdoms. Ullmann was himself a Roman Catholic and he doubtless saw in this consistency a reflection of Christ's mandate to Peter to 'Feed my Sheep', a mandate that passed through Peter to the popes. But much the same story could be told by Protestant or unbelieving historians, with the difference that these grandiose papal claims would be seen as a woeful tale of self-promotion, the usurpation of the legitimate autonomy of the secular sphere which was finally rectified in the Reformation of the sixteenth century and the secularisation that ensued.

These perspectives on papal history look for grand patterns in complex chains of events. But so long a history, stretching over two millennia and touching almost the whole world, defies neat pattern-making. There is a witty footnote in one of the wittiest works of theology published in the late twentieth century, by the Catholic priest-philosopher, the late P. J. FitzPatrick, which runs as follows:

> I have long held six figures to be the founders of the Roman Church as we know it: the Emperor Claudius, Gregory the Great, the Prophet Mohammed, Martin Luther, Napoleon Bonaparte, and Sir Charles Wheatstone. Claudius established the Roman Civil Service, which is the ancestor of the [Roman] Curia . . . Moreover, by recruiting it from the dregs of society, Claudius ensured that its loyalty would be directed without intermediary to the Imperial figure. Gregory the Great, Consul of God, as his epitaph rightly described him, was able amidst a distracting life to look westwards towards new work, rather than towards the Christian East (aided, it must be added, by his intellectual limitations: he had little understanding of classical literature and had lived for years in Constantinople without learning any Greek). As Gregory

looked west, so the rise and diffusion of Islam weakened the ancient eastern Churches. By the end of the Middle Ages there was no practical rival to Rome. The divisions of the reformation in the 1500s could not but make of the Papacy a tangible expression of adherence to the old religion, while the sweeping away of so much by the French Revolution, and the reshaping in Europe by what followed it, left the figure of the Pope isolated and dramatised in a new way altogether. . . . Sir Charles Wheatstone . . . produced the first practically usable form of the electric telegraph. Given that, Rome could be as near a bishop as could a neighbouring diocese. Communication, here as elsewhere, began to fashion what was communicated.

Breaking of Bread, Cambridge 1993, pp. 259–60

FitzPatrick was pointing in his own mischievous way to the sheer random happenstance of the historical forces that shape all great institutions, even sacred ones like the papacy. That sense of the contingency of papal history is in marked contrast to the reverential sense of timelessness with which it has often been surrounded. Since at least the fifth century the popes have claimed that their office was directly created by Jesus Christ in his own lifetime: he willed that his Church should be ruled by the Apostles and their successors, and he gave to Peter, as leader of the Apostles, the fullness of spiritual power, the keys of the kingdom of heaven. Peter came to Rome and there appointed his own successors (the earliest of whose names are recited to this day in the canon of the Mass) – Linus, Cletus, Clement and so on, down to Benedict XVI, now, as they say, gloriously reigning. All that the modern Catholic Church claims for the Pope, his authority in doctrine and his power over institutions, is on this account a simple unfolding of the dominical bestowal of the keys, and of the post-resurrection command to Peter to feed Christ's sheep.

The historical reality, of course, is not quite so simple. The most famous of all 'papal' bible texts, Matthew 16:18 – 'You are Peter, and upon this Rock I will build my Church...and I will give to you the keys of the kingdom of heaven' – is quoted in no Roman source before the time of the Decian persecution in the middle of the third century, and the very roots of what may be called the foundation myth of the papacy are uncomfortably complicated.

Christianity established itself in Rome some time in the AD 40s. Historians are now by and large agreed that for the best part of the century that followed there was nothing and nobody in Rome who could properly be called a pope. The Church in Rome emerged out of the Roman synagogues. To begin with it resembled them in being not so much a single church as a constellation of independent churches, meeting in the houses of wealthy converts or in hired halls and public baths, without any central ruler or bishop. The Jewish community in Rome had fourteen synagogues in the first century. Unlike the synagogues in other great Mediterranean cities, including Antioch, the Roman synagogues were all independent, with no central organisation or single president, and the earliest churches in Rome almost certainly also functioned independently. Many of them were in any case ethnic or regional churches – groups of Syrian, Greek or Asian residents in Rome, using their own languages, following the customs of the Christian communities back in their home regions. Elsewhere, in the first century, episcopacy emerged as the dominant form of church order – the rule of each church by a single senior presbyter who took the lead in ordinations and the celebration of the Eucharist, and who was the focus of unity for all the Christians of a city or region. But Rome – probably because of the complexity and ethnic and cultural diversity of its Christian communities – was slow to adopt this system.

Everything we know about the Church at Rome in its first century or so points to a community that certainly thought of itself as one Church, but which was in practice a loose and at times divided federation of widely different communities, each with their own pastors and their own distinctive and often conflicting liturgies, calendars and customs. But the threat of heresy within this seething diversity, and the need to impose some sort of unity and coherence on the Church, led to the acceptance of the rule of a single Roman bishop. That development was underpinned and validated by a succession narrative that expressed the Roman Christian community's pride in the life and death among them of the two greatest Apostles. As described in the first chapter of this book, by about AD 160 shrines had been built over the supposed graves of Peter and Paul, and those shrines were being shown to Christian visitors to Rome. By the early third century the bodies of the deceased bishops of Rome were being gathered into a single crypt in what is now the catacomb of San Callisto as a sort of visible family tree stretching back, it was believed, to the apostolic age. This tidying up of the past presented the tangle and confusion of real history as a neat and orderly relay race, with the baton of apostolic authority being handed from one bishop to another.

Tidiness was the keynote of this process. The earliest surviving succession list of the Roman bishops was recorded towards the

Nine third-century popes are buried in the crypt of the popes in the catacomb of San Callisto on the Via Appia Antica, a deliberate symbol of institutional continuity, as the Roman Church consolidated its apostolic pedigree.

end of the second century by St Irenaeus of Lyon, as part of a general argument that the best way to refute heretics was to refer them to the doctrine that the bishops of the great apostolic churches had received from the Apostles. Irenaeus's list started with the earliest bishop of Rome, Linus, and went up to the contemporary incumbent, his own friend Pope Eleutherius. And conveniently, this apostolic pedigree had exactly twelve names, the number of the tribes of Israel and the twelve Apostles, and the sixth was called Sixtus – or 'Mr Six'!

The emergence of the popes was a response to an unusually chaotic and diverse religious situation in the hub of Empire, a city as pluralistic as modern Chicago, New York or San Francisco. And from the beginning, the popes have been concerned above all with the achievement of unity. The first real recorded exercise of papal muscle occurred at the end of the second century, during the episcopate of the first non-Greek bishop of Rome, the African Pope Victor. It set an agenda and an orientation for the papacy that remains to this day.

The story has come down to us in rather garbled form in Eusebius of Caesarea's *Ecclesiastical History*, and his version runs something like this. Through most of Asia Minor in the late second century the churches kept Easter at Passover, whatever day of the week that fell on. The church in Rome, however, which for many years had not celebrated Easter separately at all, had settled on the Sunday nearest Passover as the appropriate day. According to Eusebius, Victor picked a row with the Asian churches, ordering them to abandon their custom and follow the Roman rule. When they refused he excommunicated them all, earning the rebuke of Irenaeus, who reminded him that earlier bishops of Rome, as a sign of fundamental unity, had sent fragments of the Eucharist to churches keeping a different date for Easter.

The story as Eusebius tells it cannot be quite right, not least because Eucharistic bread sent by boat to Asia Minor would have gone stale and mouldy long before it arrived. What we have here is almost certainly a confused account of an internal jurisdictional row in the city of Rome, where the chief elder or bishop, the first Latin-speaker to be elected to this post, evidently decided to insist on all the Christian communities in the city following a single calendar. The ethnic churches of Asian residents in Rome refused to fall into line, appealing to the apostolic customs of their home churches in Asia. The subsequent row spiralled across the Mediterranean, with the regional churches weighing in on the side of their nationals in Rome. So from its earliest appearance, the papacy has been preoccupied with the imposition of Roman order on regional diversity – and from the beginning it has been resisted and rebuked by other Christian communities and their leaders who could appeal to their own past against Rome's more authoritarian and tidy-minded present.

For non-Catholics, of course, the significance of the papacy stems not from its religious claims but from its impact on human affairs. Thomas Hobbes famously remarked that the papacy was 'not other than the ghost of the deceased Roman Empire, sitting crowned on the grave thereof'. The comment was certainly not intended as a compliment, but it encapsulated an important historical reality nonetheless. Through no particular initiative of their own, the popes inherited the mantle of Empire in the West; the papacy became the conduit of Roman imperial values and symbolism into the European Middle Ages. In a time of profound historical instability at the end of antiquity and in the early Middle Ages, the see of Peter was a link to all that seemed most desirable in the ancient world, custodian of both its sacred and its secular values. The papacy embodied immemorial continuity and offered divine sanction for law and legitimacy. So popes crowned kings and emperors and, on occasion, attempted to depose them. Even in the eighth and ninth centuries papal authority stood high, although the papacy was the prisoner of local Roman politics and many of the popes themselves were the often unlearned younger sons of feuding local dynasties.

The papacy stood outside the local entanglements of churches which were embedded in the social, political and economic structures of their societies. Submission and fealty to the papal 'plenitude of power' offered great landed institutions like monasteries exemption from the more burdensome and immediate interference (and financial claims) of local bishops. The adjudication of the popes in the countless jurisdictional, doctrinal and disciplinary disputes of Christendom was a resource appealed to by all parties. Had papal authority not existed in the Middle Ages, it would have to have been invented.

Papal claims reached their height in the central Middle Ages. Bernard of Clairvaux told his pupil, Pope Eugenius III:

> In truth there are other doorkeepers of heaven and shepherds of flocks: but you are more glorious than all of these . . . they have flocks assigned to them, one to each: to you all are assigned, a single flock to a single shepherd . . . You are called to the fullness of power. The power of others is bound by definite limits, yours extends even over those who have received power over others.

Bernard made these lofty claims in a treatise designed to teach the Pope the obligation to serve others, and to reform himself and the papacy. But the same claims were often turned by the popes into a platform from which to dominate the world. This tendency was already evident in the career of the great

The French Pope Urban II was one of the reforming monk-popes who transformed the fortunes of the papacy in the late eleventh century. In 1095 at a synod at Claremont he called on the chivalry of Europe to come to the aid of the Byzantine Church, and to 'liberate' Jerusalem from Muslim rule, thereby inaugurating the Crusades.

and forceful ninth-century pope, Nicholas I, who confronted and faced down emperors. It reached its most famous expression in the early fourteenth century with Boniface VIII, whose bull *Unam sanctam* declared that it was 'altogether necessary to salvation for every human creature to be subject to the Roman Pontiff'. Everything the modern papacy claims, and very much more besides, such as the papal deposing power, was claimed for the popes then. I discuss some of the issues here in the chapter on Pope Innocent III. In the high Middle Ages the popes most certainly shook the world. It was an eleventh-century pope who first called on the armed force of Christendom to 'liberate' the great pilgrimage sites of Jerusalem and the Holy Land from Muslim domination: the crusades were the result, inaugurating a centuries-long bloody episode whose consequences reverberate still.

In the centuries after this zenith of papal influence, the papacy went on insisting on the universality of its spiritual authority, but in reality it declined drastically, even among all the Catholic powers of Europe. The Renaissance popes could command the greatest artists and architects in Europe, and they created a Christian Rome whose glories were designed to outshine pagan antiquity, and to assert the claims of the papacy against dissent within and beyond the Catholic Church. But the spiritual claims of the papacy were complicated and, in the eyes of many, compromised by the fact that the popes all too often behaved like mere Italian princes, aggrandising their relatives (including their children) while exerting over the Church a hold which had as much dynasty as divinity about it. The rock on which the Renaissance popes founded their fortunes was not so much Christ's promises to Peter, as the papal monopoly on the mining of alum, the rare mineral essential for the tanning of leather.

Large tracts of northern Europe repudiated papal authority during the Reformation of the sixteenth century. But the papacy, which even to Catholic reformers had seemed almost hopelessly corrupt, made a startling recovery. As Catholic institutions and Catholic doctrine came under threat, the popes emerged as a

centre of continuity and a spearhead of renewal. Rome became
both the executive centre and the symbolic focus of a resurgent
and aggressive Catholic Counter-Reformation. But paradoxically,
this very resurgence of papal energy triggered a reaction among
the Catholic powers of Europe. They began to find irksome
the ancient claims of the popes to intervene in secular matters.
Popes of the time might have inhabited buildings that spelled
out an almost megalomaniac vision of papal dominance, like the
monstrous bronze baldachin that Pope Urban VIII raised over the
papal altar in St Peter's, embossed with enormous heraldic bees
from his own family's coat of arms, but in reality the popes were
in serious danger of being reduced to purely ceremonial significance. In 1606 Pope Paul V put the entire Venetian Republic
under solemn interdict for what he saw as incursions on papal
authority. Interdict was the popes' most formidable weapon, a
collective excommunication and ban that in theory halted the
celebration of any sacraments and rites – Baptism, the Eucharist,
Marriage, Christian burial – throughout Venetian territory. But
the rulers of Venice called the Pope's bluff, forcing the clergy
to carry on as usual or be banished. After a year of deadlock,
the Pope was forced into a humiliating climbdown. Underneath
the elaborate deference of the Catholic world, the papacy and
its often inconvenient religious demands were resisted. Cardinal
Richelieu said of the Pope, 'We must kiss his feet – and bind his
hands.' So the kings and queens of Catholic Europe appointed
their own bishops, taxed the clergy, policed contacts between
the local churches and Rome, restricted the publication of
papal documents, determined the syllabus in the seminaries and
expelled or dissolved the religious orders as they pleased. And in

all this the popes grumbled, protested and complied.

The modern papacy, therefore, with its unchallenged jurisdiction over the whole Catholic Church, is not the product of a steady evolution from simple beginnings, the natural growth of some essential acorn into a mighty oak. In a real sense it is, rather, the result of a historical catastrophe, the French Revolution. The Revolution swept away the Catholic kings who had appointed bishops and ruled churches, and once more made the popes seem the embodiment of ancient certainties. As can be seen from the discussion of the pontificate of Pius IX in this book, the hostile secular states that emerged in nineteenth-century Europe attempted to reduce the influence of the Church in public life, but they were happy to leave its internal arrangements to the Pope.

The most crucial and important practical power possessed by modern popes is arguably the right to appoint the bishops of the world, and thereby to shape the character of the local churches. It is salutary to remind ourselves that the popes did not possess this unchecked power in canon law until 1917, and the practice of direct papal appointment of bishops did not become general until the nineteenth century. Before then the Pope's role in appointing bishops was not generally as universal pastor but as Primate of Italy or as secular ruler of the Papal States. The 1917 Code of Canon Law itself, which lies at the heart of papal domination of the modern Church, arguably owes at least as much to the Napoleonic Code as to Holy Scripture, and the exercise of papal authority in the modern Church is rooted in quite specific aspects of the institutional and intellectual history of the last two hundred years.

Effective diplomacy and recognition of the Church's influence over more than a billion Catholics worldwide have gained the popes a unique – and sometimes controversial – voice in international affairs.

Whatever its roots and its vicissitudes, papal influence over world events remains formidable. Popes no longer mobilise armies or launch crusades, but over the last century or so a greatly enlarged papal diplomatic corps of nuncios and apostolic delegates has secured for the modern popes powerful representation to most of the governments of the world, and in international bodies like the United Nations. Catholics form a fifth of the world's population, and the Catholic Church is the world's largest conglomerate of humanitarian and relief organisations. Those facts alone give immense significance to the opinions and actions of popes.

23

It was because they knew that the words of the Pope had the power to move millions that the Allies in the Second World War were so determined that Pope Pius XII should condemn Nazi atrocities. And, with the rise of instantaneous modern communications and modern forms of travel, the popes have gained a direct and imaginative presence in both Church and world unthinkable in earlier ages. The capacity to translate that symbolic religious valency into world-shaking action was startlingly demonstrated by the crucial role of Pope John Paul II in the fall of communism in Poland and the wider Soviet bloc. For good or ill, the popes continue to shake the world.

➤➤ ◄◄

This book began life as a series of ten talks given on BBC Radio 4 in September 2007. Ten popes (nine, if one counts Peter as an Apostle rather than a pope) from a succession of more than 260 can by no stretch of the imagination be called a representative selection. My choice of popes for discussion was neither an attempt to nominate the ten 'best' nor even the ten most influential. An entirely plausible series with the same title could have been compiled with ten quite different popes as its subject matter. But each of the men discussed here encapsulates one important aspect of the world's most ancient and durable religious institution. The material on Pope John XXIII has been very slightly expanded. Otherwise, the ten talks are printed here just as delivered.

1

ST PETER

In the spring of 1939, as war loomed over Europe, workmen began digging a grave for the recently deceased Pope Pius XI in the crypt of St Peter's basilica in Rome. Three feet below the ancient floor, their spades struck the top of a substantial pagan burial chamber, which turned out to be just one in a whole street of second-century pagan tombs stretching 300 feet east and west, and disappearing directly under the high altar of the church above.

Throughout the Second World War a team of archaeologists laboured in secrecy to excavate this extraordinary street of the dead. Their digging led them at last to a small and nondescript monument wedged into a corner of the cemetery. You can still get permission to see it, but it's not much to look at when you do – about 2 metres high, it is set at an awkward angle into a red wall which once ran along an alleyway between the pagan graves. Imagine a marble fireplace flanked by single pillars and topped with a small gabled structure shaped like a temple – in fact the archaeologists called the whole thing the *aedicula*, or little temple. It became clear that the first Christian church built on this spot early in the fourth century, by the first Christian emperor, Constantine, had been designed round this *aedicula*. Constantine's engineers had literally moved a mountain to achieve this. The *aedicula* stood halfway up the Vatican hillside; the Emperor's men sliced the top off the hill and dumped the spoil – more than a million tons of it – into the valley, creating a level plain. The first St Peter's basilica was then built on top, with the high altar positioned directly over the insignificant little monument. But Constantine had moved more than earth and bricks and mortar, for you could say that not only St Peter's basilica, but the Roman Catholic Church itself is founded on this ancient piece of stonework.

We now know that the *aedicula* is an early Christian monument, erected about AD 160 to commemorate the crucifixion of St Peter in the nearby Vatican circus, under the Emperor Nero. It is mentioned in the writings of the Roman cleric Gaius who, in a treatise written at the end of the second century, spoke of the monuments to the Apostle Peter at the Vatican and of the Apostle Paul on the Via Ostiensis. 'If you will go to the Vatican', he wrote, 'or to the Ostian Way, you will find the trophies of those who founded this church.' Gaius believed that these 'trophies' were the graves of the two greatest Apostles, and there is in fact an empty grave directly underneath the *aedicula*. Scratched into the plasterwork nearby is an ancient graffito in Greek, just two words, *Petros eni*: Peter is here. The experts are still arguing about the fine detail, but whether the little monument marks the grave of Peter, or simply commemorates his execution near the spot, the *aedicula* is certainly the most ancient and the most concrete

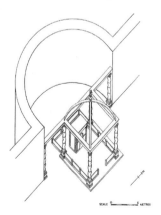

Isometric drawing of the altar and shrine over Peter's grave, as it was in the pontificate of Gregory the Great.

The martyrdom of Peter in Rome, though unrecorded in the bible, became the foundation-stone of Roman understanding of papal authority. In these scenes from a fourth-century Roman coffin, Peter cuts off Malchus' ear in the Garden of Gethsemane, and is arrested by the Roman authorities.

embodiment of the Roman Catholic claim that the leader of the Apostles spent his last years in Rome, that he was martyred there, and that the long line of bishops of Rome, the popes – all 262 of them – are Peter's successors.

Peter, whose original name was Simon Bar Jonah, is one of the dominant figures of the New Testament. He is mentioned first in all the lists of Jesus' Apostles, and acts as their leader and spokesman. He was an impulsive and warm-hearted man whom Jesus renamed 'Kephas' in Greek, 'Petrus' or Peter in Latin, meaning 'the Rock' or 'Rocky', probably a reflection both of his character and of his role as anchor-man for the other disciples. St Matthew's Gospel tells how Peter was the first to recognise Jesus as the Christ or anointed one of God, and how in return he received a special authority from Jesus:

> Blessed are you, Simon son of Jonah, for flesh and blood has not revealed these things to you, but my Father who is in heaven. And I say to you, you are Peter, and upon this Rock I will build my Church, and the gates of hell shall not prevail against it, and I will give to you the keys of the kingdom of heaven, and whatever you bind upon earth, shall be bound also in heaven, and whatever you loose upon earth shall be loosed also in heaven.
>
> Matthew 16:17–18

Those words became the foundation charter of the Roman Catholic Church, and the special proof-text for papal authority. If you stand in front of the high altar of St Peter's and look up you will see them carved in Latin letters six feet high, all round the base of Michelangelo's great dome, a triumphal canopy spelling out the momentous significance of the little shrine now so far underground.

This is all the more remarkable because Peter betrayed Jesus, just as Judas Iscariot did. The Gospels tell how Peter courageously followed Jesus into the house of the high priest after his arrest, but his courage evaporated when he was challenged by the servants, and he swore three times that he didn't know Jesus. And then the cock crowed, and Peter went out and wept bitterly. The story of Peter's denial of Jesus in the darkness before dawn is too terrible to be anything but the literal truth, but, unlike the story of Judas, it doesn't end in despair and suicide. The last chapter of the Gospel of St John tells how the risen Jesus himself forgave the penitent Peter, and reconfirmed him as leader. Appearing at dawn to the disciples by the shores of the lake, he reversed Peter's dawn betrayal by quizzing him three times, 'Do you love me more than these others do?' When the grieved Apostle replied, 'You know everything, you know I love you', Jesus appointed him chief shepherd of the Christian flock: 'Feed my lambs, feed my sheep.'

And so Peter emerged as the unchallenged leader of the early Christian movement. It was he who preached to the crowds in Jerusalem at the first Pentecost, and it was to him that a miraculous vision was granted, authorising him to baptise the pagan Cornelius, and so to reach out beyond Judaism to all the peoples of the world. And when the newly converted Paul went to Jerusalem to seek guidance from the Apostles, he tells us himself that he spent fifteen days there, consulting mainly with Peter.

So it is all the more remarkable that Peter, after dominating so many of its pages, simply fades out of the New Testament. The Acts of the Apostles, the nearest thing we have to a contemporary record, devotes most of its first twelve chapters to Peter's activities. Then, quite abruptly, it tells us that after escaping from prison, Peter had 'departed and gone to another place'.

And that's the last we hear of him. The rest of the New Testament offers just two clues to Peter's eventual end: the risen Jesus in Chapter 21 of John's Gospel declares to Peter that in old age 'you will stretch out your arms and another will bind you and take you where you do not want to go', a prediction, John tells us, of the manner of Peter's death – in other

Moritur ad terram verſo capite in cruce Petrus.

The crucifixion of Peter in Rome was a foundational event for the theology of the papacy. In this Jesuit depiction, that point is made by the presence of the dome of St Peter's on the skyline of first-century Rome!

words, a reference to the early Christian belief that Peter, like Jesus, died on a cross. And the First Epistle of Peter, which may or may not be based on the Apostle's own teaching, is said to be written from 'Babylon', an early Christian code-name for Rome, where the writer clearly thought that Peter, like Paul, had ended his life.

If the New Testament offers us only hints and coded references to Peter's ultimate fate, however, from the end of the first century onwards a growing stream of early Christian writing makes clear that it was taken for granted that Peter had indeed come to Rome, and that he and Paul had been martyred in Nero's persecution in AD 65. Tradition has it that Paul, who was a Roman citizen, was beheaded with a sword, while Peter died the excruciating death on the cross reserved for slaves and low-class foreigners, and that their martyrdom in Rome established the two men as joint patrons for the Christians there. So the Epistle of St Clement, written to Christians at Corinth on behalf of the Church at Rome around AD 90, refers to Peter and Paul as '*our* Apostles'.

There was far more to this than just an interesting fact about historical origins. The highest claim any early Christian community could make for itself was that it had been founded by one of the Apostles. Apostolic teaching and apostolic witness by martyrdom remained as a presence and a power within the communities in which the Apostles had lived and died, shaping their character and development, anchoring them in the witness of the first disciples of Jesus. And almost as soon as a Christian literature begins, we find the Church at Rome claiming, and other churches conceding, that the Christians at

Rome had the unique privilege of not one but two Apostles for their founding fathers.

The monument underneath St Peter's is the strongest single piece of evidence we have that the claim was rooted in historical fact, that the Christian community at Rome did indeed preserve the memory of Peter's death and burial among them, recorded not on paper or parchment, but in bricks and mortar in the corner of a pagan graveyard. But if its small scale and poor materials are clues to the social status of most of the first Roman Christians, the *aedicula* is also the symbolic pivot of a great shift in human history.

The grave of Peter and the beliefs he died for embodied an understanding of religion that was entirely alien to Roman civilisation. For pagan Rome, the worship of the gods was about the handling of power and the management of luck: the gods embodied the energies that dominate human life – war, sex, the elements and the seasons and, perhaps especially in Rome, the State, with its divine emperor and its demand for total loyalty. Worshipping the gods involved not the inner transformation of heart and mind, but the performance of certain prescribed external actions – making a sacrifice, honouring an image. It had almost nothing to do with what we now think of as the heart of religion – morality, the separation of truth from falsehood, the search for the meaning of life. Those were matters for the philosopher, not for the priest or the worshipper. The polytheism of Rome had the inclusiveness of domination, a sort of symbolic scalp-collecting, notching up another people conquered, another religion in the list of cults to which temple space might graciously be allowed – the more the merrier, provided none of it interfered with real life, with the supremacy of Rome and the pursuit of power.

For the monotheism of the Jews the gods were so much poison, the subjugation of humanity to its basest instincts, the worship of sex, beauty, luck, irrationality, power and all the other forces that distract, torment and enslave us. The God of Israel was not some tribal mascot demanding blood, but the wisdom that had made the universe, the power of good and evil that underlay all moral action, the embodiment of the justice and compassion that made human life bearable. These were powerfully attractive ideas, and Judaism did draw converts, but its unbreakable links to Jewish history and Jewish identity prevented it from becoming a truly missionary religion. By parting company with the syna-gogues that had sheltered it, Christianity shed that restriction. The notion of the one and only God who is the antithesis and annihilation of all the gods had taken shape within Israel, within a single people's history: Christianity was the vehicle that took that wisdom to the world. It invited men and women of every race and colour to a new and deeper understanding of religion, the worship of a God of goodness, rationality, truth and self-sacrificial love.

By the time of Peter's death, his colleague Paul was groping his way towards a theology that spelled out the identification of that God of goodness, rationality, truth and compassion with the wandering rabbi Jesus, with whom Peter had walked the roads of Palestine, and whom he had loved, and denied, and loved again. The location of those mighty abstractions within a single human life, vividly recorded in the Gospels and profoundly reflected on by thinkers like Paul, was an idea whose moment was come. In the centuries that followed it would capture the imagination of a world sick of the grotesque antics and inhuman demands of the gods, a world hungry for light and hope and mercy where death and darkness and amoral power seemed always triumphant. The Christian faith in Nero's reign, when Peter was crucified, looked like yet another tribal absurdity, but it was destined to banish the superstitions, to shake down the walls of pagan Rome itself and to rebuild them in the service of the God and Father of Jesus Christ. At the shrine of Peter in the red wall under the Vatican we stand at a threshold, one of those rare fault lines opening out between one age of the world and the next.

2

LEO THE GREAT

440–461

Rome lies at the heart of Roman Catholicism. Not just the city itself, the ancient capital of the world and the residence of the popes, but the Rome of the imagination, the spiritual centre to which all roads lead. Roman Catholicism is the largest of all Christian churches, and so Rome is in some sense the spiritual home of more than a billion Christians, scattered across the globe.

Given the origins of Christianity, this religious centrality of Rome is a very surprising development. Not only did Jesus never set foot there, but he was crucified by a Roman imperial army of occupation. In the First Epistle of St Peter and in the last book of the New Testament, the Book of Revelation, Rome features under the code-name 'Babylon' as the great whore, the idolatrous murderer of the saints. Peter himself was one of the saints whom Rome murdered, along with his colleague Paul. Their graves there might easily have become a standing witness to the incompatibility between the pagan Empire and the followers of Jesus. Instead, they became the foundation stones of a Rome reshaped and re-imagined as a Christian Holy City.

Leo the Great, Pope from 440 to 461, was the key figure in this transformation. The Emperor Constantine had adopted Christianity early in the fourth century, hoping its strong religious and moral teaching would be an ideological glue to bind together the scattered people of an empire stretching from Britain in the west to Syria in the east. Constantine himself abandoned the city of Rome and moved the capital of Empire to Byzantium, renamed Constantinople, on the Black Sea, but over the next century or so the bishops of Rome, the popes, became the city's most important citizens, leading the way in reshaping it as the capital of the emerging Christian world. Wealthy citizens were buried in stone coffins decorated with bible stories instead of scenes from pagan mythology. Church buildings invaded the ancient pagan civic spaces, the praises of the martyrs recorded on them using the monumental script once used to celebrate the victories of emperors and armies. Their mosaics portrayed the Apostles as senators in togas; Christ was depicted with the features and attributes of Apollo or Jupiter. The most brilliant scholar of the fourth century, St Jerome, was commissioned to produce a new translation of the bible in up-to-date Latin, so that God and his holy Apostles could speak out plainly, as Romans to the Romans.

But all this might have remained a matter of mere surface and presentation, an oriental religion got up in Roman dress, if Leo the Great had not developed a distinctively Roman theology, an account of why Rome mattered that made sense in specifically Christian terms.

Leo had been elected Pope after proving himself as a brilliant ecclesiastical administrator and diplomat, but he was far more than a pious bureaucrat. He emerged as a great preacher in sermons for the feast days that had replaced the old pagan festivals, above all at the midsummer feast day of Saints Peter and Paul on 29 June. In them, Leo gathered together the ideas about the meaning of history and of Rome itself which had been evolving for more than a century, and welded them into a powerful new theology.

Rome was beloved of God, he told his congregations, not merely because it had once been the capital of the Empire, but because it had been the centre of God's plan for the salvation of the world. Yes, the pagan empire had been founded in blood and deceit and the worship of false gods, but God had permitted Rome to become great so that the Christian Gospel might journey down the roads of Empire. Ancient Rome, Rome of the fables, had been founded by the heaven-blessed twins, Romulus and Remus. Christian Rome, Rome of the truth, had been re-founded on a far greater pair of heavenly twins, the Apostles Peter and Paul. They had baptised the city in their blood, and now in heaven they were still Rome's teachers and protectors. Unlike the old Rome, this Rome could never die, for its power and authority were rooted not in brutality, but in the grace and truth of God.

> Behold, thanks to Peter, you have become head of the world: you reign over a vaster empire by virtue of divine religion than ever you did by earthly supremacy.

And if Christian Rome flourished under the protection of the Apostles, the city's bishop, the Pope, held a special authority as the representative and spokesman of Peter, Prince of Apostles. However unworthy he might be, each pope was the heir of the Apostle: Peter acted and spoke through Leo.

> And so if anything is rightly done and rightly decreed by us, if anything is won from the mercy of God by our daily supplications, it is because of his work and merits whose power lives on and whose authority still prevails in his See.

Leo was a practical man, and he translated his conviction of the supreme dignity of the Church of Rome into action, persuading the Emperor to recognise the Pope's supremacy over all the other churches of the West. He directed a stream of letters to churches in Italy, Gaul, Spain, the Balkans, Africa and Greece, concerned with everything from clerical appointments and efficient Roman ways of organising church life to the best remedies for divisions and schisms. He encouraged, instructed and rebuked other bishops in concrete expression of the 'plenitude of power' which he believed that the Pope, and only the Pope, had inherited from Peter.

But for Leo the privileges of the papacy were neither a matter of clerical bureaucracy nor an end in themselves. They were designed above all to protect the truth of the Christian creed. He declared:

> The Lord shows a special care for Peter and prays in particular for the faith of Peter, as if the future would be safer for others, if the spirit of the leader remains unconquered. So in Peter the faith of all is strengthened.

At just this time, the faith of Christendom was in turmoil throughout the Greek East, where some of the most fundamental Christian beliefs were being contested. Christianity proclaimed that in Jesus, God himself had taken human flesh and had died to redeem the world. Jesus was the son of Mary; he was also the Son of God. But how *could* the same individual be both human and divine, the eternal all-powerful creator of the world *and* a mortal man who had sucked milk from his mother's breast and bled to death on the cross?

The Christianity of the Latin West was muscular and down to earth, concerned with clean living and plain thinking, not much given to speculation. In the more subtle and sophisticated East, however, conflicting theories about the divine nature leaked out of the lecture halls and libraries into the pubs and market places, and were regularly debated there, sometimes with the help of fists and broken bottles. One particularly influential theologian, Eutyches, came up with the theory that in Jesus the human and divine natures had somehow been fused into a unique single new nature, higher than merely human, a little less than fully divine. This idea was eagerly adopted by many, violently repudiated by others. Conflict became so widespread and ferocious that it seemed to threaten the stability of the Empire itself. In 451 the Emperor summoned a great Council of bishops at Chalcedon to settle the matter. Flavian, the Bishop of Constantinople, worried that Eutyches' views might win out, appealed to Leo to exercise Rome's ancient role as referee of contested doctrines.

Leo responded with a short theological treatise, nicknamed 'the Tome', which is almost certainly the most important document ever issued by a pope. A brilliant distillation of the no-nonsense conservatism of Latin Christianity, the Tome restated the paradoxes of the New Testament in starkly simple yet eloquent language. All talk of a mixed nature in Jesus, Leo insisted, was just a poisonous muddle which turned the Son of God into some sort of monstrous hybrid. Jesus was indeed a single person, but in him two natures, human and divine, coexisted without confusion and cooperated for the salvation of the world. Jesus was perfectly human, but he was also fully divine – 'complete in what belonged to him, complete in what belonged to us'. Otherwise, *our* humanity could not have been redeemed and made immortal, and we would still be in our sins. The Church must faithfully proclaim this wonderful mystery, the reality of a

The early Councils of the Church were convened by emperors and no pope ever attended one. But the western Church came to believe that Councils were illicit unless called or endorsed by the Pope. In this fanciful seventeenth-century image of the Council of Chalcedon, Pope Leo presides in person over the assembly.

loving God whose incarnation was 'a stooping down of pity, not a failure of power', giving us a saviour whose human nature truly wept for the death of Lazarus, and whose divine nature raised Lazarus from the dead.

The Tome of Leo, read out to the bishops at Chalcedon, was immediately recognised as a consummate summary of the ancient faith of Christendom. Its powerful clarity, saturated in the language of the New Testament, cut through all the complex webs of abstract speculation, and the Council hailed Leo's intervention as literally heaven-sent. 'Peter has spoken through Leo.' Fifteen hundred years on, the Tome of Leo remains the touchstone of mainstream Christian teaching about the Incarnation.

For Leo, the Council's enthusiastic expressions of gratitude were a matter of course. Naturally they accepted his words as the words of Peter – was he not Peter's heir and spokesman? For the eastern bishops and theologians assembled at Chalcedon, however, matters were not so simple. All of them recognised that from time immemorial Rome had functioned as a court of appeal for doctrinal disputes, and in Pope Leo's Tome they recognised an inspired expression of their shared beliefs. But not all of them accepted Leo's exalted sense of his own office: they hailed his words because they recognised them as true, not because they came from the Pope.

And in any case, the Council's gratitude had a sting in the tail. To please the Emperor they issued a ruling which outraged the Pope: they recognised the special dignity of the Bishopric of Constantinople, new Rome, because it was the imperial capital, just as old Rome had once been the imperial capital.

For Leo there was far more at stake here than a matter of polite precedence. The authority of the Bishop of Rome did not come from the political history of his city, but from the blood of the Apostles Peter and Paul. To honour Constantinople as new Rome was to confuse spiritual and political authority, and he rejected the Council's decision outright.

In this quarrel the later divisions between the eastern and western churches were ominously foreshadowed, and so also were many of the conflicts between Church and State in the

European Middle Ages. Already the papacy was drawing a sharp line between the authority of the Church and the authority of even a Christian secular ruler.

Leo's reign as Pope coincided with the waning of Rome's greatness. With the Emperor far away in Constantinople, Rome's military and economic might was crumbling and barbarian armies had begun to invade the Italian peninsula. In 452 Leo led a successful embassy to Mantua to persuade Attila the Hun not to attack Rome. (In later Roman legend, illustrated on the baroque carving on Leo's tomb in St Peter's, Saints Peter and Paul themselves supported Leo and terrified Attila.) Three years later, however, a Vandal army captured Rome and looted it. Every church in the city lost its communion vessels, and Leo was forced to melt down the lavish gold and silver ornaments of his cathedral, Constantine's own gifts, to equip the parishes with the bare essentials for Mass.

But if he presided over the twilight of Rome's secular glory, Leo also laid the foundations for the subsequent development of the papacy. He helped establish the spiritual dignity and freedom of human beings by rejecting any equation of political and spiritual power. And though it would be another fourteen hundred years before papal infallibility was defined, all its essentials were already implicit in the 'Tome' he addressed to the bishops at Chalcedon. It is hardly an exaggeration to say that Leo invented the papacy as we know it.

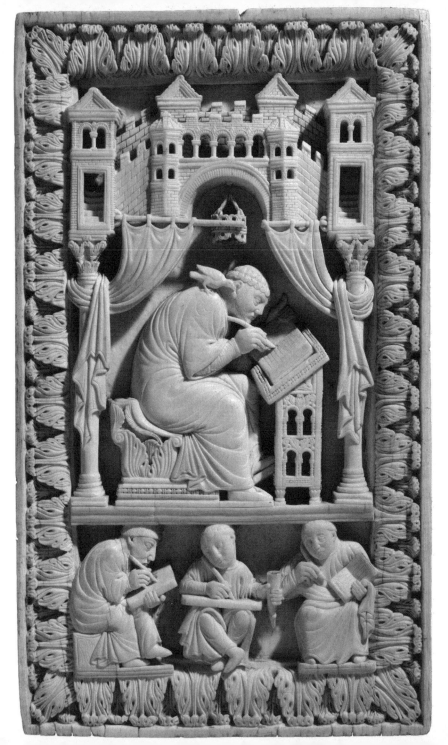

3

GREGORY THE GREAT

590–604

Whenever a new archbishop of Canterbury is enthroned, he makes his solemn vows touching a battered Gospel book, copied somewhere in Italy more than fourteen centuries ago. Its text is handsomely written, though the few surviving illustrations are drawn in a comic-strip style that makes *The Beano* look sophisticated.

This venerable piece of flotsam from the wreck of the Roman world almost certainly came to England in the luggage of a papal mission sent to the kingdom of Kent in the year 596. Christianity had been widespread in Roman Britain, but it had been swamped by successive waves of heathen invaders from Germany, the people whom we know as the Anglo-Saxons. In the early 590s Pope Gregory the Great, the first monk to be elected Pope, became curious about the tall, fair-haired pagan English captives he saw for sale in the Roman slave markets, and he despatched a group of forty fellow monks to preach the Gospel to these handsome men and women from the world's end. He is rumoured to have quipped that these people who called themselves Angles in fact looked more like angels.

Gregory's initiative for the conversion of the English is remarkable, for in Italy he was coping with what must have looked like the collapse of civilisation, or even the end of history itself. 'The world grows old,' he declared in one of his sermons, 'it hastens towards its death.' He could be forgiven for thinking so. The Rome he ruled as Pope was no longer the million-strong capital of the world it had been. Over the previous two centuries war, disease and famine had decimated its population to fewer than fifty thousand. The emperors had long since moved east and ruled from Constantinople, the 'new Rome' (modern Istanbul).

Rome's great theatres, basilicas and palaces were crumbling into ruins, and the aqueducts that had fed its baths and fountains leaked uselessly into the surrounding countryside. Northern Italy was under the boot of the Lombards, barbarian tribes from Austria who had swarmed into the peninsula while Gregory was still in his teens. Less than a generation on, they had seized Milan, the former imperial capital, and were knocking at the gates of Rome. The Byzantine emperors still demanded the loyalty – and the taxes – of the people of Italy, and an imperial exarch nominally ruled Italy from Ravenna on the Adriatic coast. But he was too weak and too far away to offer any practical protection to the beleaguered citizens of Rome.

Gregory watched all this with anguish. The eldest son of an aristocratic family with a long record of office in Church and State, he had been educated for power and service. There were two popes among Gregory's extended ancestry, and in his early thirties he served as prefect of Rome, the city's executive mayor, a demanding job in which his younger brother would follow him. People of Gregory's class, however, were losing confidence in Rome's secular greatness. They looked instead to the Church and its message as the only source of true happiness in a falling world, increasingly their preferred outlet for talent. Gregory's widowed mother and three of his aunts all became nuns, and once his stint as city prefect was completed, Gregory handed over his estates in southern Italy and Sicily to the Church, turned the family mansion on the Coelian Hill into a monastery and served there himself as an exemplary monk.

For the rest of his life Gregory would look back with yearning on his years of monastic seclusion, study and prayer, 'when I rose in contemplation above all changeable and decaying things, and thought of nothing but the things of heaven'.

But he was not left alone with the things of heaven for long. The popes of the sixth century were harassed men, responsible for victualling the city, keeping the Lombards at bay by bravado or bribery, finding money to pay what imperial troops there were, ransoming captives, and feeding and clothing the growing hordes of refugees and the native Roman poor. Pope Benedict I, at his wits' end with all this, hauled Gregory out of his retreat on the Coelian Hill, ordained him deacon and put him in charge of the Church's charitable work. Gregory proved so efficient that Benedict's successor, Pelagius II, appointed him to the key post of papal ambassador at the imperial court. In Constantinople, Gregory maintained a semi-monastic routine of study and prayer, preaching to his household the great series of devotional sermons on the Book of Job, which was destined to become one of the most influential books of the Middle Ages. But he was also a networker, making crucial friendships that stood him in good stead as Pope, not least with the royal family (he became godfather to the Crown Prince). Gregory was recalled to Rome after six years to become Pope Pelagius's chief adviser. When Pelagius died in the plague that swept through the city in the wake of devastating flooding in 589, it was inevitable that Gregory would be elected to succeed him.

Almost nine hundred of Gregory's letters survive, so we know more about his pontificate than that of any other pope of late antiquity. The range of his activities, the grip and minuteness of his tireless involvement in the myriad responsibilities of the greatest bishopric in the Christian world are astonishing even in

Gregory's treatise 'On the Pastoral Care' established itself as a textbook for all in authority, secular as well as sacred. This translation of Gregory's work into English was made by King Alfred the Great, and is open at the King's prefatory letter.

our time of global expansion. His concerns stretched from Visigothic Spain and eastern Gaul to Africa, Greece and the Balkans. His letters show him organising corn supplies from Sicily to feed the famine-stricken people of central Italy; enforcing clerical celibacy; overseeing the administration of the papal horse ranches; rebuking bishops who were mistreating Jews or who could not get on with their senior clergy; buying the liberty of Roman citizens enslaved by the Lombards; overhauling the administration of papal lands to eliminate corruption; securing trusted Roman clerics, especially monks, for vacancies in provincial bishoprics; defying imperial legislation designed to prevent men of military age from becoming monks; sending gifts of relics or sacred books to encourage pious princes; cultivating the Catholic wives of pagan or heretical rulers, even among the Lombards, whose souls, as a bishop, he wanted to save (though, as a proud and aggrieved Roman, he loathed them).

Yet not all of this pleased the Romans, especially not the Roman clergy. Gregory's generosity relied heavily on his family's wealth, but his emphases on charity and clerical celibacy were characteristic concerns of a monk, and the Roman clergy didn't much enjoy having this austere and energetic monk making new demands on them.

Despite Rome's prestige, the Pope had not yet acquired the unchallenged authority that Gregory's medieval successors would take for granted, and he often had to depend on persuasion and the force of his own personality. This could create conflicts, most fiercely when he discovered that the Patriarch of Constantinople, as bishop of the imperial city, was using the title 'ecumenical' or 'universal' patriarch. Little more is likely to have been intended by this than to register the special relation of the Patriarch to the capital of Empire, but Gregory saw Constantinople's claims not only as an assault on the ancient primacy of Rome, but also as a denigration of the other patriarchal sees of Antioch, Jerusalem and Alexandria. He tried, not entirely successfully, to persuade these other patriarchs to join him in opposing Constantinople's pretensions. They evidently failed to understand why he was so upset by the matter, the Patriarch of Alexandria even addressing a letter to Gregory himself as 'Universal Pope'. Gregory reacted with horror. 'I beseech your holiness', he wrote, 'never call me that. Titles are not the measure of real greatness, but rather the quality of our lives. Whatever is exaggeratedly attributed to another is taken away from you. Nothing honours me if it undermines the honour of my brothers. My honour is the honour of the universal church. So away with these words which puff up vanity and wound charity.'

Gregory was a Roman aristocrat to his fingertips: his reaction proceeded in part from outrage at any challenge to the primacy of the see of Peter. But he also sincerely believed that all authority, including his own, must be rooted in humble service, not in marks of status. He coined the self-description 'Servant of the servants of God'. Later popes would adopt this as a papal title; few lived up to it as he did. But though he meant what he said about humility, the title also contained a sly insistence on the primacy of Rome.

There was no master plan, no overarching strategy for Gregory's many enterprises. He was a resourceful man who responded with intelligence and energy to the multiple crises of his times. But his mission to England would in the long run create a master narrative and transform the way the papacy itself was understood. It is not entirely clear why Gregory decided to send his monks to England – he may have thought he was recovering a former Roman province for Christian civilisation – but whatever the reasons, the conversion of England became the defining

British divisions over the dating of Easter and other issues were resolved in favour of the Roman practices at the synod of Whitby in AD 664, though all trace of the buildings in which the synod was held have long since disappeared.

event of Gregory's pontificate, and one of the foundations of the medieval papacy itself. As a matter of fact, monks from Ireland played at least as large a role in Christianising England as anyone Gregory sent, but it was the papal mission and Gregory's initiative that eventually gave the Anglo-Saxon Church its sense of identity. Roman customs, Roman liturgy, Roman saints, even Roman tunes for chanting the psalms became for the English the measure of authentic Christianity. Back in Rome, Gregory's memory would be allowed to fade. But in England he was 'Gregorius noster', *our* Gregory. His treatise 'On the Pastoral care', a how-to-do-it manual for bishops, became the model not only for English bishops, but the pattern for the exercise of all authority, including that of the King. The first full-length biography would be written not in Rome, but by an English monk in the monastery at Whitby.

Gregory took a close personal interest in the progress of the mission and sent calm and commonsensical letters of guidance to the sometimes hyper-anxious monk Augustine whom he had chosen as first archbishop. Their subjects ranged from how new converts should modify their sex life, to what prayers ought to be used at Mass. Some of Gregory's advice went to the very heart of mission itself: he at first advocated a policy of zero tolerance towards pagan religion, the destruction of all temples and the denunciation of the pagan gods as demons. But he changed his mind, advising Augustine instead to purify the temples and then turn them into churches, to adapt the pagan festivals as celebrations of the Christian mysteries and Christian saints, to emphasise continuities rather than confrontation.

For the newly Christian English, Rome was unique, the fountainhead and source of all truth and wisdom, the Pope the founder and father of their faith. In due course, missionaries from England would take the Gospel as Gregory understood it to the pagan lands of north-eastern Europe – Boniface to Germany, Willibrord to Holland. They would carry with them their intense reverence for Rome, and would look to Gregory's successors for authority and guidance.

Within a generation of Gregory's death in 604, the followers of his younger contemporary, Mohammed, had begun that great sweep across the eastern and southern Mediterranean that would eventually overwhelm the ancient churches of Africa and Asia Minor. The Mediterranean itself would cease to be a Christian lake. But as one world passed away, another was coming into being. Increasingly cut off from the Byzantine Empire, the popes would turn north and west, and the new Christian nations there would turn to them. Struggling to hold back the collapse of the classical world, this aristocratic Roman monk had unwittingly invented Europe.

Gregori⁹ vij

4

GREGORY VII

1073–1085

For a hundred years or more, most western countries have worked on the axiom that our common life together ought to be deliberately secular. Religion in a free society may be acceptable as a private activity, like knitting or going to the gym, but it has no proper place in the spheres of politics, economics or citizenship.

The rise of militant Islam, like the influence of the Christian Right on American foreign policy and, perhaps more encouragingly, the role of the Catholic Church in the overthrow of Polish communism, might suggest that in the real world things are not necessarily quite so simple.

That much at any rate was understood in the Middle Ages, where everyone accepted that religion – the fundamental understanding of life, death, the Universe and everything – was liable to have an impact on the way that society was organised. Furthermore, for almost a thousand years the Church was deeply embedded in every social structure. The bishops and abbots of the great monasteries were powerful landowners, commanding armies of tenants and dependants, deploying vast resources and sitting alongside barons in the councils of kings. Schools, universities, hospitals and orphanages were founded, inspired or managed by the Church. Religion was as inescapable as the church towers that dominated the local landscape, pointing the way to heaven but resting on solid, earthly foundations.

If the Church impinged on the world, the world also impinged on the Church. The Church was rich, so men who cared little for Christ's message still wanted a slice of the action. Wealthy families endowed charities for their souls' sakes, but they also jostled to have their sons made bishops and abbots, to tap the Church's

The reform movement of the tenth and eleventh centuries brought the papacy increasingly into conflict with kings eager to exploit the power and wealth of the church. This illustration from a twelfth-century chronicle depicts the struggle of Pope Gregory VII with the 'emperor' Henry IV.

wealth and influence. The distinctions between prayer and profit became blurred. Religious office was bought and sold. The clergy were supposed to be celibate, set apart for God's work, but in practice many had common-law wives or were legally married, and were as preoccupied as anyone else by material anxieties and family ambitions, and just as liable to corruption.

From these entanglements not even the papacy was exempt. Central Italy was in political chaos at the end of the first millennium and the popes were forced to rely on powerful families around Rome to protect and enable their work. Since there is no such thing as a free lunch, the result was a century of aristocratic nonentities appointed pope by local Mafiosi. Most of these popes were mediocre; some were very bad indeed. The papacy retained symbolic prestige as custodian of the heritage and tomb of Peter, but its moral stature shrunk as it dwindled to an insular Italian possession.

All that changed for ever in the year 1046 when the German king, Henry III, came to Rome to be anointed Holy Roman Emperor. The popes had invented the Empire two and a half centuries earlier to recruit a powerful ruler as God's policeman. The Emperor was charged with suppressing the Church's enemies and promoting its work of education and conversion. In return he received the prestige of divine sanction for his rule in the shape of solemn papal coronation.

Henry III took this role as protector of the Church to unprecedented heights. The earnest German king was appalled by the squalid state of the papacy, and concerned that his own legitimacy as Emperor would be undermined if he were anointed by a suspect pope. So he deposed the Pope and put in his place an edifying German bishop. Popes were short-lived in those days; over the next ten years Henry appointed four such German popes, all men of moral stature, all zealously committed to the reform of Church and society. In a five-year whirlwind pontificate, the greatest of these German popes, St Leo IX, who also happened to be the Emperor's cousin, went a long way towards reviving the glory days of papal prestige. He travelled tirelessly to northern Italy, France and Germany to hold reforming synods, attacking corruption wherever he found it, deposing bishops and archbishops who had bought their jobs and asserting papal authority as it had not been asserted for centuries. Within a generation a new breed of pope had seized control of the reform movement.

In this moral and institutional renewal one man played a unique backstage role. His name was Hildebrand. Hildebrand was the son of Tuscan peasants, but he had been educated in one of the strictest Roman monasteries and was devoted with a convert's passion to the Church and Bishopric of Rome. He was also dedicated to the reform of the Church. He had seen the imperial court in Cologne and had lived as a monk in a reformed monastic house in France, probably at Cluny. Most importantly, as Archdeacon of Rome he served a succession of holy popes with titanic energy as ideas-man, cheerleader and enforcer. By 1073, when Hildebrand himself was elected Pope, as Gregory VII, he *was* the reform movement, and over the next twelve years he would shake Europe to its foundations, as he pushed the logic of a new vision of an aggressively proactive papacy to its ultimate conclusions.

Gregory VII identified three issues as key to the Church's corruption: the sale of sacred office, the marriage of priests and, above all, the interference of powerful laymen in clerical appointments. If the Church could not choose its own leaders, free from such interference, it would always remain tangled in the web of politics and money, never able to promote priests fit and willing to preach a demanding Gospel to a reluctant world.

As Pope, Gregory pursued relentlessly what one historian has called the 'moral rearmament' of Latin Christendom, a comprehensive campaign to restore the Church, the bride of Christ, to her original purity. He summoned bishops, priests and monks from all over Italy and beyond to a series of twice-yearly synods in Rome. Gregory used these synods to map out the reforms, which participants were then expected to implement in their own regions: the purging of unchaste clergy, the ordination of devout and competent priests, the abolition of the sale of sacred things and offices. He targeted the laity too, attacking corruption among lawyers, administrators and merchants, and planning a more regular and demanding use of the sacrament of confession as a means of converting minds and hearts.

Gregory believed himself to be God's watchman, charged with responsibility for the whole Church. He despatched hundreds of letters to bishops and secular rulers – to Iceland, Denmark and Sweden, where he tried to ensure the support of the monarchy for the clergy; to Hungary, where he tried to consolidate a succession of Christian kings loyal to Rome in a country newly converted from paganism; to North Africa, where he tried to protect the rights of Christian minorities in Muslim territory.

The tone of these letters was seldom conciliatory – Gregory had an exalted sense of his office as Vicar of St Peter. An extraordinary document among his papers, the so-called *Dictatus papae*, or aphorisms of the Pope, indicates the radical direction of his thinking:

That the Roman pontiff alone can depose or reinstate bishops.

That of the Pope alone all princes shall kiss the feet.

That it may be permitted to him to depose emperors.

That a sentence passed by him may be retracted by no one.

That the Roman Church has never erred; nor will it err to all eternity.

That the Roman pontiff, if he have been canonically ordained, is undoubtedly made a saint by the merits of St Peter.

That he may absolve subjects from their fealty to wicked men.

These ideas were reflected in Gregory's actions, leading the German bishops to complain that he bossed them around like bailiffs on his estate.

And it was a German king who tested this vision of the papacy to breaking point. The Emperor Henry III had launched the reform movement with a purge of the papacy, but that purge, of course, and his subsequent appointment of four popes, was itself a blatant example of lay interference in clerical matters, Gregory's greatest hate. The purity of Henry's intentions and the calibre of the popes he appointed excused *his* actions, but when his son, Henry IV, tried a repeat performance with less exalted motives, Pope and King came eyeball to eyeball, with disastrous consequences for both.

The German kings ruled northern Italy. For years, reforming popes had supported radical criticism of the unreformed Church establishment in Lombardy, and encouraged lay people there to refuse the sacraments from married clergy or from those who had bought their positions. In the resulting tensions Milan Cathedral was burned down. Unsurprisingly, the Lombard bishops resented this encouragement of anarchy and looked to

Henry IV's humiliating penance at Canossa became for European statesmen and intellectuals an enduring symbol of overweening papal ambition; hostile depictions like this one helped fuel moves in the nineteenth century to control and reduce the influence of the contemporary Catholic Church.

the King for support. In 1075 Henry IV intervened in a dispute over the succession to the Archbishopric of Milan: he sacked both candidates and appointed his own man, without consulting the Pope. The German monarchy now appeared as the enemy, not the activator, of papal reform.

Gregory VII's disastrous alliance with the
Normans of southern Italy ended in his death
and exile in Salerno, in whose cathedral he
is buried.

Predictably, Gregory threatened Henry with excommunication and deposition from his kingship; equally predictably,
the King retaliated. In 1076 he summoned a synod of German
bishops to Worms. They obediently denounced Gregory as a false
monk and declared him deposed from the papacy. But Henry

had overplayed his hand: the popes had grown in stature since the days when his father could hire or fire them like private chaplains. The German princes seized on Henry's excommunication as an excuse to shake off royal authority, issuing an ultimatum threatening rebellion unless he made his peace with the Pope within a year. Forced into a humiliating climbdown, in January 1077 Henry travelled to Canossa in the Italian Apennines where Gregory was staying for Christmas. The most powerful monarch in Europe stood, barefoot and penitent in the snow, until the Pope reluctantly absolved him and the political unity of Germany was saved. It was eloquent proof that no Christian king could rule in defiance of the Pope, and that kings indeed might have to bow to kiss the Pope's foot.

But Gregory's victory at Canossa was soon undone. The German princes rebelled anyway, electing their own king. In 1080, Gregory, unable to resolve his long-term differences with Henry, excommunicated him and declared him deposed, predicting his imminent death for good measure. Henry declined to oblige, however, and the world, which by and large had applauded the Pope's victory at Canossa, now saw Gregory as the aggressor, supporting opportunist rebels against their anointed king. Henry invaded Rome and installed the Archbishop of Ravenna as a rival pope, Clement III, who duly crowned him Emperor in St Peter's. Gregory fled south and appealed for help from the Norman rulers of Sicily. Little better than pirates, they eagerly invaded Rome, burning, raping and pillaging. Gregory was not restored and died in 1085 at Salerno, reviled by the suffering Romans, defeated, but utterly untroubled by self-doubt: 'I have loved righteousness and hated iniquity: therefore I die in exile.'

The conflict at Canossa would haunt the political imagination of Europe for centuries. To nineteenth-century Protestant politicians like Bismarck, it embodied the overweening claims of a power-mad Church, a humiliating defeat for the autonomy of the secular world that must never be repeated. But if Gregory's inflated claims do indeed look alien now, his attack on the unlimited power of monarchy has a more modern ring. Henry's bishops were shocked by the Pope's actions because they thought that kings ruled by divine right, and reverenced their very word as law. Gregory would have none of this: divine right belonged to the realm of the spirit. Like every other earthly institution, monarchy had to be fit for purpose. If they proved untrue to that purpose, kings could be set aside.

> Who does not know, that kings and rulers are sprung from men . . . who by pride, robbery, and murder . . . have striven with blind greed to dominate over their equals, that is, mankind?

Gregory was defeated in the short term, but he changed the world all the same. Other popes would avoid such all-out confrontation, but never again would the Church accept the right of kings and rulers to determine spiritual matters. Whatever Gregory's intentions, a lasting line had been drawn between the claims of conscience and the claims of state power. And under this overbearing autocratic pope, human freedom took one small, uncertain step forward.

5

INNOCENT III

1198–1216

Power corrupts, and absolute power corrupts absolutely. A century after it was first coined, Lord Acton's gloomy aphorism still speaks to our deep-seated contemporary suspicion of power and the powerful. But is it always true?

Power and its entanglements have haunted the history of the papacy because for much of the Middle Ages the popes were, quite simply, the most powerful men in the world. And the most powerful pope of the Middle Ages was Lothar of Segni, who became Pope Innocent III in 1198.

Innocent was born to power: he was the favoured son of an aristocratic Roman family, and he had the best education money could buy – theology at the University of Paris, law at the University of Bologna. So far as we know he was the first pope to have had a university education. He was a cosmopolitan man – as a student he even visited England, to see Thomas Becket's shrine at Canterbury. And when he was elected Pope at the age of only thirty-seven, he brought to the papacy not only one of the sharpest minds of his generation, but also that very rare thing in a pope, the abounding energy of youth.

The institution Innocent inherited was power incarnate – a major player in world politics and one of the richest corporations in existence. For more than a century the popes had struggled to make the German emperors obedient supporters of the Church and papal policy, and by 1200 they seemed to have succeeded: Innocent got his own candidate, Otto IV, elected Emperor, and when he turned out badly, deposed him and had him replaced with another candidate of his choice. He intervened vigorously in the politics of Norway, Sweden, Bohemia and Hungary, and when King John of England refused to accept his appointment of a friend from university days, Stephen Langton, as Archbishop of Canterbury, Innocent put the whole country under solemn excommunication. The King capitulated, and even made England a fiefdom of the papacy, recognising Innocent as his feudal overlord.

The rulers of Europe accepted the Pope's right to these extraordinary interventions because politics was, quite literally, a matter of life and death. Kings went to war, executed criminals, levied taxes which might oppress the poor: these were moral choices – they involved sin and salvation. As a priest, the Pope might have no direct say in the affairs of this world, but wherever sin and salvation were in question, he was supreme. Innocent applied to himself and his office a text from the prophet Jeremiah: 'I have set you over nations and over kingdoms, to pluck up and to break down, to destroy and to overthrow.' And so, he believed, the Pope was set between God and man: 'He judges all, and is judged by no one.' Previous popes had called themselves 'Vicars of St Peter' – St Peter's deputy. Innocent was the first pope systematically to use the title 'Vicar of Christ'. The ideological stakes had been raised.

Political involvement meant bloody hands, and Christ's vicar could and did summon armies. In the eleventh century, Pope Urban II had invented the idea of crusade: Christian knights took vows as pilgrims, abandoned home, family and the blessings of peace, and went to war to liberate subject Christian populations living under Islamic rule, and to free the holy places in Jerusalem for pilgrimage. Crusading captured the imagination of Christian Europe. It offered the ruling classes, soldiers by profession, a road to salvation, not *despite* their warlike way of life but precisely in return for their involvement in a paradoxical new concept, a *holy* war.

Innocent saw nothing wrong in the use of force to achieve a holy outcome, and he pushed crusading into new areas. The crusade ideal had always been justified as a form of legitimate self-defence, a struggle on behalf of oppressed Christian peoples. But Innocent now blessed armies engaged in the forcible conversion of pagan populations in northern and eastern Europe, where there was no plausible plea of self-defence. And more notoriously, he blessed the crusade against the Cathars of southern France.

The Cathars denied the central doctrines of Christianity: they were dualists, who taught that the material world was evil, the creation of the devil, and that salvation came through the soul's escape from the contamination of the body. The doctrine of the Incarnation, therefore, teaching that God had taken flesh, was a demonic lie. Marriage, sex and procreation were evil because they trapped new souls in the prison of the flesh; the sacraments of the Catholic Church, which used material signs as vehicles of the sacred, were bad. In a world in which human life was all too often nasty, brutish and short, these lurid views about the horror of bodily existence struck a chord, and Catharism made many converts in southern France. Innocent sent personal representatives to investigate, and when his legate was murdered by Cathar guerrillas, the outraged Pope author-ised a crusade, taxing the French clergy to pay for it. But the crusading commanders, and the French crown that recruited them, were more interested in territorial conquest and finan-cial gain than the salvation of souls. In the bloody campaign that followed, the region was raped and plundered, and whole towns slaughtered indiscriminately. For a while, Catholic orthodoxy prevailed, but at a terrible price.

Crusading armies even turned against Orthodox fellow Christians. The beleaguered Byzantine Empire appealed to the West for help against the advance of Islam. The Pope called on the chivalry of Europe to rescue the Greek Christian civilisation, and an army recruited from all over Europe set out for the Middle East. But a power struggle was in progress for the imperial throne in Byzantium, and one of the contenders invited the crusading army to intervene. Centuries of distrust and mutual misunderstanding between Orthodox and Catholic Christians meant that many of the crusaders considered the Greeks almost as bad as the infidel they were fighting. In 1204 the army recruited to defend it was turned on the greatest city in the Christian world: Constantinople was looted, its treasures, relics and icons dispersed, the population terrorised and butchered.

Pope Innocent was appalled, and denounced the sack of the city as soon as he heard of it. But he too distrusted the Greek Church, and he soon saw the overthrow of Byzantium as a sign from God. He installed a Latin patriarch loyal to Rome in Constantinople, and authorised the systematic westernisation of the Greek Church. It was a shameful and catastrophic error of judgement. Greek memories of western treachery in their hour of need would persist for centuries, and still poison relations between Orthodox and Catholic Christians today.

If the Pope was the arbiter of European politics, he was also the head of a vast financial corporation. Over the centuries the churches had accumulated treasure, and in an age where the gulf between rich and poor was growing, and large-scale urban destitution was on the increase in the towns of the Mediterranean, clerical wealth provoked reaction. Catharism had appealed in part because its teachers often lived lives of great austerity, travelling barefoot, eating only vegetables and abstaining from sex.

All over western Europe, lay religious movements emerged that emphasised gospel poverty and were hostile to institutional complexity and clerical greed. These movements, modelled on the wandering life of Christ and his Apostles, were often led by uneducated laymen who preached without episcopal licence from unauthorised translations of the bible. Unsurprisingly, their teaching was often weird and could tip over into downright heresy. For the followers of such movements, the institutional church had made a devil's compact with power and privilege. For the clerical authorities, anarchy, ignorance and error were rampant, disguised as evangelical poverty.

This was a potentially disastrous polarisation. Much of the religious zeal and creativity of medieval Christianity was seeking expression in these movements, but all that zeal and creativity was in danger of being forced outside an official church, compromised by its entanglements with the world of power and wealth.

That the polarisation was halted is largely due to the imagination and insight of Pope Innocent. Until now the popes had viewed the new movements with undisguised hostility, but Innocent saw that condemnation was not enough: spiritual hunger had to be fed, legitimate aspirations had to be met. He recognised the dawning of a new age of lay Christianity, which would become the Church's enemy if it was not catered for. From the start of his papacy, he tried to meet the new movements halfway. Instead of condemning them he allowed them to operate, provided

The dream of Innocent III, in which a ragged poor man supported the collapsing Church of Rome, was claimed by both Dominican and Franciscan friars as a prophecy of the role of the mendicant orders in the renewal of the Church in the thirteenth century.

they stayed within the bounds of official doctrine. During the crusade against the Cathars, persuasion had been tried as well as persecution, and a group of wandering Catholic preachers had emerged in southern France, led by a Spanish monk, Dominic Gutzmann. Dominic recognised the appeal of the austere life of the Cathar evangelists, and so his preachers too backed their Catholic preaching by dedicating themselves to absolute poverty. And Pope Innocent saw, understood and approved.

Then in 1210, a group of twelve ragged men appeared in Rome to ask for his blessing. They were led by an eccentric dropout called Francis Bernardoni. The spoiled son of a wealthy cloth merchant from the hill town of Assisi, Francis had been overwhelmed by growing pity for the abject destitution of the poor living all around him. In a visionary moment that would transform the art as well as the religion of Christian Europe, he identified the poor with the naked Christ on the cross. Jesus was the ultimate social victim, the ultimate pauper, and whoever would follow Jesus must likewise strip himself bare of possessions and give his life to the service of the poor. This was not a message that came naturally to a man of Innocent's aristocratic background and cast of mind, yet once again he saw, understood and approved. He tonsured Francis and his little band of laymen, making them clerics and so subject to episcopal control. But he also gave them permission to preach love and repentance, provided they steered clear of theology. The Franciscan movement had begun.

The Pope's recognition and protection made all the difference to the followers of Dominic, men of the mind, and the followers of Francis, men of the heart, and both movements spread like wildfire. Pope Innocent's approval gave form and influence to movements that might otherwise had drifted away into mere protest, and within a generation the friars, as they were called, had injected into official Christianity a new intellectual vitality and religious ardour. Absolute power, which might have snuffed them out, had instead been used to create space for the most dynamic religious forces of the Middle Ages.

Innocent met lay religious aspirations in less spectacular but

PIAZZA
INNOCENZO III

The little hill town of Anagni was the birthplace of three medieval popes: Innocent III, Gregory IX and Boniface VIII, whom Dante placed head down in a furnace in Hell.

hardly less momentous ways. At the Fourth Lateran Council in Rome in 1215 he steered the bishops of Europe towards a new framework of local pastoral care which would remain the fundamental structure of western Christianity into modern times. The Council decreed that every man and woman should receive communion at least once a year after confessing their sins to their local priest. In turn, those priests must be educated so that they could instruct the people adequately, and inspire them by example. The Council provided a core curriculum covering all the fundamentals of the faith. Elementary as all this sounds, this was the first systematic pastoral framework of its kind, and it established new and higher expectations for the parish clergy. They were no longer to be just the village shaman, but teachers and spiritual guides as well.

Charisma and structure: they don't often combine, but when they do they are unstoppable. Innocent was a man of his time – shrewd, savvy, energetic, a man who understood power and was not afraid to use it. He was no saint, but he knew a saint when he met one, and if he used the greatest moral authority the world has ever known to wreak havoc on the Church's enemies, he also used it to make room for the saints. Without vision, says the prophet, the people perish. And just for once, absolute power had been wielded to make room for the visionaries.

6

PAUL III

1534–1549

By the start of the sixteenth century, the papacy was Europe's most important institution, the court of final appeal in tens of thousands of lawsuits, a centre of patronage and raw power. Imagine the EU headquarters, the United Nations and the International Court of Human Rights all rolled into one, and you begin to get the idea. And then add the World Bank, because in many ways the Pope and cardinals had become more like the chief executives of a global business corporation than priests of the Christian Gospel. Some of them, of course, were pious and conscientious; more were grizzled and experienced diplomats and power brokers. Wealth and power often made them forget their vocation – you didn't have to be a priest to be a cardinal, and many had mistresses, and families turning into dynasties. They were also important patrons of art, science and learning: the world's best writers, painters and philosophers flocked to Rome to mop up some of the wealth swilling through the courts of the Pope and his cardinals.

The sophisticated Mediterranean world was prepared to live with these contradictions, with high priests of God who were also gang bosses and *bons viveurs*. But in the more earnest and anxious north, men and women were scandalised. In 1517 a German monk named Martin Luther, disgusted by the sordid fund-raising campaign launched by the Pope to pay for the lavish rebuilding of St Peter's, staged a public protest. Luther began with a straightforward attack on corruption, going on to deny fundamental ideas about sin and salvation that had underpinned the structures of western Christianity for a thousand years. Luther and his followers put the text of the bible against the traditions and teaching of the Church, and they rejected most of the Catholic sacraments along with the authority of pope and priesthood. The Protestant Reformation had begun. Within twenty years, Germany and central Europe were in turmoil, and religious war was looming everywhere.

The popes were slow to grasp the seriousness of all this. Clement VII, Pope through the 1520s and early 1530s, was a respectable enough priest, but he was also the bastard son of the great and cultured Medici family of Florence, and had succeeded an uncle as Pope. As a cultivated aristocrat he simply couldn't take seriously a vicious theological squabble in the wilds of Germany. And so the most powerful religious revolution for centuries gathered momentum almost unopposed, and the serious-minded and the devout increasingly looked to Protestantism rather than to the Catholic Church to meet their spiritual longings.

In 1534 the cardinals chose a new pope. The election of Alessandro Farnese, who took the name Paul III, must have come as proof that the penny still hadn't dropped about the need for reform. A member of one of Rome's most opulent families, he had become a cardinal in the first place only because his sister Giulia was the mistress of the reigning Pope, the notorious Alessandro Borgia. The wags of Rome referred to Cardinal Farnese as 'Cardinal Pettycoat'. He maintained a handsome mistress of his own, by whom he had four children. As cardinal, Farnese built a stupendous palace on the Via Giulia and filled it with expensive art treasures. Titian painted him three times, each portrait better than the last, capturing an extraordinary character with long, muscular hands, piercing, clever little eyes under beetle brows and a patriarchal beard bristling with a vitality that belied his age. He was sixty-seven when he became

Farnesiorum palatium.

The Villa Farnese, whose *piano nobile* was designed by Michelangelo, was the great dynastic palace built by the future Pope Paul III: a centre of extravagant display, it is an emblem of the worldliness and sophistication of the Renaissance papacy.

Pope, and he was determined to make the most of it. He immediately appointed two grandsons, aged fourteen and sixteen, as cardinals, and made his son commander-in-chief of the papal armies (though he was to prove less than a credit to the Pope – there were rumours of a homosexual rape from which the victim died).

Paul was the last of the partying popes: he shocked prudes by reviving the Carnival; he won the hearts of the Roman crowds by paying for bullfights and horse races in the streets; he gave lavish dinners for the glitterati in the papal apartments. More enduringly, he commissioned Michelangelo to redesign the civic centre of Rome on the Campidoglio – making what is still one of Rome's most beautiful public spaces – and to complete the decoration of the Sistine Chapel with a stupendous Last Judgement. He also appointed the seventy-two-year-old artist as architect for the new St Peter's, one aged titan's homage to another.

But if this looked like Rome fiddling while the Church burned, appearances were deceptive. Even in Renaissance Rome the spirit of reform was stirring, and Paul himself had been touched by it. Long before he became Pope he had pensioned off his mistress and begun to live a celibate life, and in 1519 he took the unusual step of having himself ordained priest, a sign of deepening religious seriousness. Under the extravagant display there were hidden depths. As soon as he became Pope, and despite the shameless aggrandisement of his family, he began to appoint cardinals from outside the traditional recruiting ground of high politics and papal diplomacy. These were zealous, devout men, committed to the root and branch reform of the Church. They included a pious young member of the English royal family, Reginald Pole, Henry VIII's cousin, who had been groomed by the King to become Archbishop of Canterbury, but was now in permanent exile for his outspoken criticism of Henry's divorce and break with Rome. In 1535 Paul made another Englishman a cardinal, Europe's greatest Catholic theologian, the Bishop of Rochester, John Fisher. Fisher was a prisoner in the Tower of London at the

time because of *his* opposition to Henry VIII, and Paul probably hoped to save his life, thinking Henry would never dare
kill a cardinal. In this, as it turned out, he was mistaken.

But Paul pressed on with reform. One of his new cardinals
was an earnest Venetian nobleman called Gasparro Contarini,
who had been through a religious conversion like Luther's
many years before, and was now a rallying point for Catholic
reformers. Paul asked Contarini to head a commission of like-
minded men to analyse what needed to be done to clean up
the Church. Their report was a bombshell – a catalogue of
corruption and failure from the Pope downwards, so devastating that Martin Luther rushed out a German translation as
propaganda for the Protestant cause.

Paul's reforming cardinals soon separated into two schools of
thought. The group that formed around Contarini and Pole was
deeply shocked by Protestant rejection of pope and sacraments,
but they considered Luther to be right in preaching the help-
lessness of human beings without the grace of God: however
wrong-headed and rebellious Protestantism might be, it had a
better grasp than the official Church on this almost-forgotten
aspect of the Gospel. But another of Paul's new brooms,
Cardinal Giampietro Caraffa, violently disagreed. A fierce
Neapolitan, ablaze with southern passion channelled entirely
into religion, Caraffa was of the opinion that any suggestion
that the Protestants might have a point amounted to treason.
The only way to deal with heretics was to hunt them down
and either convert or kill them. He persuaded Paul to establish
the Inquisition in Rome with himself as its head. He then
began to compile an index of prohibited books for burning and

cultivated a ring of informers with eagle eyes for any hint of softness towards the Reformation. When he himself eventually became Pope in 1555, he would turn on his former colleagues in reform, rounding up and arresting members of the soft Left who had formed around Contarini and Pole.

But that was far in the future. For now, Paul allowed repression and renewal to go forward together. The revitalisation of religious life was in the air. In 1542, Pope Paul gave his approval to the constitutions of a new religious movement led by a diminutive Spanish war veteran, Ignatius Loyola. The Society of Jesus, the Jesuits, would rapidly become the most vital force within the Catholic Church, an international elite of highly educated and totally dedicated men, inevitably dubbed as the storm troopers of the Counter-Reformation. They would take a renewed and fighting Catholicism back into the areas of northern and eastern Europe colonised by the Reformation, and wherever they went they rolled back the revolution. Even more momentously, they would lead the mission to convert civilisations that had never known Christianity – in the Americas, India, Japan, China, whole worlds to east and west which exploration was opening up. And the Jesuits were the forerunners of a century-long flowering of new religious orders, dedicated men and women committed to practical action as well as contemplative prayer.

Ever since Luther had first preached his new Gospel, people on both sides of the confessional divide had been calling for a General Council of the Church to thrash out the issues and instigate reform. Paul's predecessors resisted these calls, in part at least because it was inevitable that item number one on the

Paul III approved the Constitutions of the Society of Jesus, founded by the Catalan soldier Ignatius Loyola: within a generation, the Jesuits would become the cutting edge of a resurgent Catholicism.

agenda of any such council was liable to be the reform of the papacy. But Paul saw that the bullet had to be bitten and in 1545, after endless delays and political manoeuvring, the Council met at Trent in the Italian Alps. It would last, on and off, for the next twenty years, and Paul did not live to see its most momentous decisions. But the Council clinched the reconstruction of the Catholic Church. Paul put the leftward tendency under Cardinal Pole in charge, but the moment for reconciliation had passed. In the event, the Council decided against any opening towards Protestantism, and instead sharpened and defined traditional Catholic teaching on every contested question. But it also legislated for the practical transformation of structures – properly trained priests who didn't have mistresses, bishops who stayed in their dioceses and worked to educate and reform, monks and nuns who led edifying lives of prayer and penance. A new, energetic, better-informed Catholicism would emerge, with a creed which could inspire.

The new Catholicism was much more serious – it was also much less fun, and decidedly narrow-minded. Writers patronised by Paul and his predecessors would be banned by the popes who came after him; papal craftsmen would construct bronze fig leaves to cover the glorious nakedness of the statues he commissioned. A new puritanism had entered Catholicism and it had come to stay, for Paul's reforms had made the inclusion of people like himself impossible. The popes of the later sixteenth century were by no means all saints, including as they did other aristocrats with an eye for extravagant display, but Paul's successors had at least to *try* to look like more conventional priests, and there would be no more grandsons among

CONCILIVM TRIDENTINVM.
Velut expressum est in ade Cathedrali D.Mariæ sacra

The Council of Trent, dominated by Italian bishops and papal influence, refused all compromise with the reformers, but gave the Catholic Church both a clearer doctrinal basis and a blueprint for practical reform.

the cardinals. In a century that would end with religious wars between Catholics and Protestants, the careless confidence of the Renaissance had given way to something more earnestly didactic, and more deadly.

For Paul had fostered energies that would feed both the confidence and the killing. His search for renewal and reform had set in place creative forces that would help the Catholic Church re-establish its intellectual bearings and its Christian credentials. But he also gave room and respectability to a repressive mentality that tried to conserve the truth by force. Catholics, and the rest of the world, have been living with those energies ever since.

N.S. PÈRE LE PAPE PIE IX

259ème Successeur de St Pierre

7

PIO NONO

1846–1878

The papacy is the oldest dynasty in the world. When it was born the Roman Empire was young; since then civilisations have come and gone, but the succession of the popes has endured. The Church has worked with, and survived, whatever political arrangements have come along.

But the arrival of democracy almost destroyed it. With the coming of the French Revolution in 1789, the fundamental values of western democracy received their decisive expression: in politics, the rule of the people rather than of kings or aristocracies; in religion, freedom of conscience; in civic life, equality before the law regardless of race, colour or creed.

In theory Catholic Christianity has no quarrel with these noble ideals; indeed, many of them evolved out of Christian affirmations about the dignity and equality of human beings before God. In reality, however, the Catholic Church's actual experience of the birth of democracy was not as enlightenment and liberation, but as a murderous attack on religion in general, and the freedom of the Church in particular.

For the French Revolution quickly became anti-religious: Christianity was banned in France, church property confiscated, holy places desecrated, priests and nuns murdered. When French revolutionary armies invaded Italy, Pope Pius VI was kidnapped and died a prisoner in France, and men called him the last of the popes. Later, when Napoleon seized control of the Revolution, he stole the treasures of the Vatican and imprisoned the new Pope, Pius VII, in solitary confinement in France, hoping to turn him into a puppet-pope who could be wheeled out to bless the Corsican's imperial ambitions.

The popes survived both the Revolution and Napoleon, but

they never forgot these terrible experiences. Behind the high promises and idealistic slogans of liberty, fraternity and equality they heard the voice of atheism, murder and theft. In the first half of the nineteenth century the papacy identified the survival of Christianity with the restoration of strong government and the rejection of the modern world. The toughest-minded pope of the nineteenth century, Gregory XVI, wouldn't even allow railways into the Papal States.

Then in 1846 the cardinals elected a pope who seemed altogether less fearful, less clenched against modernity. Giovanni Mastai-Ferretti, who took the name Pius IX, Pio Nono in Italian, was one of the most likeable popes ever elected. He was devout, kindly, unstuffy and at ease in the company of women (there were vague rumours of romantic irregularities earlier in his life, which didn't necessarily do him any harm in Italian opinion). At fifty-five he was the youngest pope for centuries, and his reign was to last for thirty-two years, longer than any other before or since. He loved to meet people, he had a boisterous sense of humour, he looked like everybody's uncle, and he frequently stained his white cassock with the snuff he endlessly inhaled. His predecessor, Gregory XVI, had suspected him of being a dangerous liberal, and he was elected because the cardinals, after a harsh and intolerant papacy, wanted a change. In his early years as Pope, Pio Nono was a moderniser: he reformed the government of the Papal States, bought himself a railway train, removed the worst disabilities of the Roman Jews, and he generally thought of himself as a go-ahead Victorian (he revered Queen Victoria and deluded himself that she might one day become a Catholic). And he was an ardently patriotic Italian who wanted the end of

Austrian rule in the peninsula. So Italians adored him, cheering him whenever he appeared in the streets; young Romans would even take the horses from between the shafts of his carriage and pull it along themselves.

He was a pope of the people, the first pope of the mass media. Cheap print and photography made his face familiar in every Catholic home and, in the age of great new shrines like Lourdes, he presided over an unprecedented surge in popular Catholicism. This resurgent piety took practical forms. Pio Nono fostered a huge growth of the religious orders, tens of thousands of idealistic men and women who devoted themselves to running schools, hospitals, orphanages, a great outpouring of self-sacrificing and largely unpaid social work on a scale quite new in world history. This was global Christianity, Christianity for the age of empire and expansion, Christianity for the democracy. Judged by such criteria, he was the most successful pope ever.

And yet he was no thinker: he was a poor judge of character, and even his admirers considered him rather dim. Simple-hearted and decent himself, he had an unerring knack of choosing advisers who were neither simple nor decent, such as his corrupt and worldly secretary of state, Cardinal Antonelli, a careerist who never became a priest, who practised celibacy only episodically and who scandalously abused his office to enrich himself and his brothers.

And Pio Nono had the bad luck to be Pope during the Risorgimento, when idealists and revolutionaries were fighting to end foreign domination of the Italian peninsula and to hammer it into political unity. Some liberal Catholics dreamed of an Italian federal state presided over by the Pope, but this

ITALY IN ROME.

Papa Pius (to King of Italy). "I MUST NEEDS SURRENDER THE *SWORD*, MY SON; BUT *I KEEP THE KEYS!!*"

The annexation of the Papal States and the city of Rome by the new Italian State under King Victor Emmanuel II in 1870 marked the end of more than a millennium of the temporal sovereignty of the popes.

was never a serious possibility. In fact the Papal States, straddling the centre of the Italian peninsula and ruled by a priest-king, formed the biggest single obstacle to Italian unification. Furthermore, to unite Italy the Pope would have had to declare war on Austria, which occupied much of the country, yet how could the universal pastor of all Catholics go to war against a Catholic nation? As he hesitated over this insoluble problem, Italians felt betrayed. Revolutions broke out all over Europe in 1848. In Rome, Pio Nono's liberal prime minister was murdered by revolutionaries, and the Pope himself had to flee for his life.

He even considered moving the papacy to Malta, and his whole outlook was permanently embittered. Though he recovered Rome in 1850, little by little papal territory was captured and incorporated into the emerging Kingdom of Italy until, in 1870, Rome itself was invaded, becoming the capital. Deprived of the last shreds of his temporal power, Pio Nono became the (self-imposed) Prisoner of the Vatican. He refused to recognise the new State of Italy, and he refused the compensation offered by its government, since to accept money would be to acquiesce in the theft of his territory.

Pio Nono was not wrong to be worried. The popes had ruled the Papal States for more than a millennium and the papacy's political independence was (and still is) considered by most Catholics to be essential for the free and effective exercise of the Petrine office. How could the Pope be the father of the worldwide church if he were subject to the laws of an aggressively secular State? Many of the makers of the new Italy, like Garibaldi, were hostile to Christianity, and the Pope was horrified by the State's growing and sometimes aggressive claims to responsibility for education, the family and public morality, areas in which the Church had always had a decisive say.

At every fresh invasion of the Church's prerogatives, Pio Nono issued denunciations. In 1864 Vatican draftsmen gathered these denunciations into the notorious 'Syllabus of Errors', a ragbag of eighty denunciations that included the repudiation of rights of free speech and religious liberty, and ended by denying that the Pope could or should reconcile himself with 'progress, liberalism, and recent civilisation'. 'Recent civilisation', of course,

CARDINAL NEWMAN.

The future Cardinal, Blessed John Henry Newman, deplored the dogmatic extremism of Pio Nono's pontificate: 'It is not good for a pope to live 20 years', he wrote, 'he becomes a god, and has no-one to contradict him.'

taken in context, meant quite specifically the hostile actions of the State of Italy, but the Syllabus was universally perceived as an all-out attack by the papacy on the foundations of any modern society. Horrified liberal Catholics found themselves silenced and shamed. In the atmosphere of crisis and confrontation, theology withered and Catholicism was increasingly equated with uniformity; the hold of the papacy over every aspect of the Church's life grew stronger. Many Catholics were appalled,

The convening of the First Vatican Council, which met in the shadow of the annexation of Rome by Victor Emmanuel, was the last great manifestation of Papal Rome.

convinced that the Church needed a dialogue with the modern world, that it should approve what was good and help to rectify what was bad. Mere condemnation was a cop-out. The greatest Catholic thinker of the century, John Henry Newman, deplored the increasingly confrontational mindset: 'We are shrinking into ourselves, narrowing the lines of communion, trembling at freedom of thought, and using the language of dismay and despair at the prospect before us.'

But the tide was with Pio Nono: the beleaguered Pope presided over a huge growth in the authority of his office. This was the age of industrialisation, of prosperity *and* destitution on a scale never before witnessed, the age of the Communist Manifesto. As ancient certainties crumbled in the face of revolutionary social and economic realities, the papacy seemed to many people to be the one solid rock in a sea of change. Against the flux of modernity, God had erected a bulwark behind which men and women could shelter. And so, as papal territory shrunk, papal authority expanded.

Pio Nono shared these beliefs. For him, as for thousands of souls troubled by the brutal realities of modernity, the infallible papacy was God's antidote to the universal collapse of value. He came to judge all Catholics by their attitudes to this single issue, treating any doubts about it as personal disloyalty, and he convened the First Vatican Council to secure its definition. To begin with he paid lip service to the notion that the Council Fathers should be left free to make their own minds up, but he rapidly became an impatient campaigner for the definition, 'my dogma' as he called it. Bishops who spoke against the definition were hauled over the coals. The Vatican archivist innocently allowed scholarly opponents of the definition to consult documents in the Vatican library. He was summoned before the Pope, shouted down as disloyal and stripped of his post. 'You are not one of us,' the Pope told him, 'you cannot have the keys.'

Pius IX's papacy helped lock the Catholic Church into a confrontation with the modern world from which it did not recover until the Second Vatican Council, and not entirely then. The theological rigidities of his kind of Catholicism helped

L'ILLUSTRAZIONE ITALIANA

Lire 25 l'anno. – Centesimi 50 il numero.   Anno V. – N. 8 – 24 febbrajo 1878   Fratelli Treves, Editori Milano.

ESPOSIZIONE DELLA SALMA DI S. S. PAPA PIO IX NELLA CAPPELLA DEL SACRAMENTO IN S. PIETRO. (Disegno dal vero del signor Dante Paoloccl).

Pio Nono was much loved, and much hated. Devout crowds flocked to venerate his body as it lay in state, but patriotic Roman mobs tried to throw the coffin into the Tiber on its way to the basilica of San Lorenzo for burial.

sterilise Catholic theology and social thought for generations, and his angry repudiation of the new Italy led to a suspicion of democracy in general which was to have disastrous consequences in the age of the dictators.

And yet, hindsight is cheap. It was Pio Nono's misfortune to be Pope during a time of unprecedented political and intellectual turmoil. No pope since Gregory the Great had faced so daunting a set of challenges. A subtler and cleverer mind might have fostered a deeper and less confrontational theology; a more pragmatic politician might have been able to come to terms with the terrifying dismantling of the territorial arrangements which had safeguarded the papacy's freedom of action for a thousand years. But Pio Nono was neither clever nor a pragmatist. He was a pious and impetuous man, emotional and prone to panic, caught in a political and moral earthquake, surrounded by advisers who told him he was God's trumpet against the apostasy of the age, and who urged him on to extremes. His moral vision was informed by a profound pessimism about modern secular values, which the horrors of the twentieth century as well as the experience of the French Revolution might seem to vindicate. And he is proof, if proof were needed, that even the representatives of ancient dynasties, even the popes, have no choice but to be men of their times.

S.S. Pio XII

8

PIUS XII

1939–1958

C an the Vicar of Christ be a cautious diplomat? Must the Church always call evil plainly by its proper name, whatever the consequences? Can its priests keep silent in the face of abomination, in the hope of rescuing something positive from chaos, or so that tyranny may bear down a little less cruelly on those who must endure it?

These were the dilemmas confronting Eugenio Pacelli, Pope during the Second World War, a diplomat who found himself sitting in the seat of prophecy. His reputation has suffered more than that of any pope of modern times because of his answers to those agonising questions.

In the nineteenth century the popes were confronted everywhere by governments indifferent or hostile to their claims. They resorted to diplomacy, to treaties, called Concordats, giving national governments guarantees about Catholic loyalty, even allowing them a say in the choice of bishops. In return, the Church was allowed, within limits, to get on with its life. Fighting its corner in a tough political world, the Vatican came to judge regimes primarily by how they treated Catholics. Concordats in theory were about securing freedom for the Gospel: in practice that often meant protecting the interests of the Church.

Vatican diplomacy could also be altruistic. During the First World War, a diplomat pope, Benedict XV, devoted great skill to a selfless objective – the restoration of harmony among the nations. Preaching universal peace, he struggled to preserve the impartiality of the papacy, refusing to denounce specific war crimes but urging the combatants to observe international law, hoping that all sides would see him as an honest broker, and resolve their differences by his arbitration rather than by the horrors of modern warfare. The combatants pressed him to condemn enemy atrocities; when he refused he was accused of callousness and moral indifference. Germans thought him pro-French, the French called him 'The Bosche Pope'.

Benedict died in 1922, but his vision of world peace achieved by impartial papal arbitration had made a deep impression on Monsignor Pacelli, and would inspire his own actions as Pope during the Second World War. But though their policies were similar, the wars in which they pursued them were not: idealistic impartiality in Benedict would come to look like moral cowardice in Pius XII.

Eugenio Pacelli had been born into the Roman business aristocracy: his grandfather was the banker who rescued the Vatican's finances after the fall of the Papal States. Pacelli himself, ordained in 1899, went almost immediately into the Vatican diplomatic service. Austere, reserved, intensely devout, he never worked in a parish or held a pastoral position of any kind, and to the end of his life he was a man who rarely confided in others, preferring the company of his pet canary. But he was a natural diplomat – charming and sympathetic in conversation, fluent in six languages and discreet to the point of secretiveness. In 1917 Benedict XV sent him to Munich as nuncio to Germany where he remained until 1930 – through Germany's defeat, through an abortive communist revolution that confirmed his life-long hatred of socialism, and through the turmoil and decadence of the 1920s. And in 1934 Pacelli, now cardinal secretary of state to Benedict's successor, Pope Pius XI, negotiated a Concordat with the Nazi regime, designed to ensure maximum freedom for the Church in an increasingly authoritarian state.

Pacelli loved Germany and German culture, but he despised Nazi violence and the Nazis' open hostility to the Church. He knew they would dishonour the Concordat but felt that it would at least provide a legal basis for protest when they did. The legal basis came at a price, for the Nazis demanded that the Catholic Centre Party, the main defender of the Church's interests in German politics for half a century, should be dissolved. The Nazis would have destroyed the Centre Party anyway, with or without the Concordat, and that no doubt was part of Pacelli's calculation, but the Vatican's agreement to its demise seemed to many an ominous indication of the Church's lack of enthusiasm for democratic politics.

Pacelli's boss, Pope Pius XI, was certainly no democrat: he saw communism as the ultimate enemy of Christianity, thought democratic governments too weak to resist it and, in one unguarded moment, he hailed Mussolini as a man of destiny. Nazism, however, he loathed from the start as pagan thuggery, becoming increasingly disgusted by Nazi racial policies and by the harassment of the Church in Hitler's Germany. In 1937 he issued an encyclical in German, *Mit Brennender Sorge*, denouncing Nazi attacks on the Old Testament, and infringements of the Concordat. To Hitler's fury, this 'battle call against the Reich' was smuggled into Germany and read from the pulpits. The Pope was planning another encyclical condemning racism and anti-Semitism when he died in February 1939. With world war looming, Pacelli, known for his intelligence and diplomatic experience, was elected Pope after only three ballots, in the shortest conclave for centuries. He took the name Pius XII.

Pius XI had admired and trusted Pacelli absolutely. The two

Pius XI's German-language encyclical *Mit Brennender Sorge* mounted a blistering attack on Nazi racial theory and anti-Semitism: its principal draftsman was Cardinal Michael von Faulhaber, Germany's most outspoken Catholic bishop.

men were united in their loathing of Hitler, and the secretary of state had played a key role in drafting *Mit Brennender Sorge*. But temperamentally the two men were poles apart: Pacelli had no unguarded moments, and instinctively recoiled from the confrontational stance of the encyclical. There would be no confrontations under his management.

With the outbreak of war, reports of atrocities began to come in from bishops and Vatican diplomats in occupied territory. The Archbishop of Warsaw, Cardinal Hlond, fled to Rome where he pleaded for a papal condemnation of the Nazi invasion of Poland. Thousands of Polish Catholic priests and religious died in concentration camps, but the Pope issued no condemnation.

In 1940 Germany invaded Belgium, Holland and Luxembourg. The Pope sent telegrams of condolence to all three monarchs but didn't mention the Germans, nor explicitly condemn the invasion itself.

The Pope knew of mass deportations of Jews from all over Nazi Europe. The papal nuncio in Turkey, Angelo Roncalli, told the Vatican that these deportations, allegedly to work camps, were actually to extermination. Both Roncalli and the Budapest nuncio issued thousands of bogus baptismal certificates to Jews so that they could claim the protection of the Concordats. In private the Pope expressed his horror at the deportations. Nuncios sent diplomatic notes, some of which saved Jewish lives by halting deportations, and the Pope himself issued statements deploring in general terms breaches of international law and the sufferings of innocent victims of war. But despite pressure from the allies, from local bishops, from members of the papal diplomatic corps and from within the Vatican itself, Pacelli drew back from naming names, or directly blaming the Germans. He told the Archbishop of Cologne that it took 'superhuman efforts' to keep the Church 'above the strife of parties'.

In 1942 Catholic bishops in France and Holland denounced the deportation of Jews. Pacelli was well aware that by contrast his silence dismayed many, who felt that he was abdicating the Church's responsibility to speak for the oppressed. At Christmas that year he decided he could be silent no longer, but the condemnation, when it came, was characteristically guarded and oblique. Towards the end of his Christmas Eve broadcast he lamented the fate of 'hundreds of thousands, who, through no

THE MOST CONTROVERSIAL
BESTSELLER OF OUR TIME
THE DEPUTY
BY ROLF HOCHHUTH
The full, uncut text of the
explosive drama complete with the
author's sidelights on history
FOREWORD BY DR. ALBERT SCHWEITZER

Rolf Hochhuth's 1963 play portrayed Pius XII as a 'heartless, money-grasping pontiff', a Nazi sympathiser, and an anti-Semite: the play was grossly unfair, but the moral and historical issues it raised have never gone away.

fault of their own, and sometimes only because of their nation-ality or race, have been consigned to death or slow decline'. There was no explicit mention of either Jews or Germans. For the rest of his life the Pope believed that this coded utterance was an unequivocal and outspoken condemnation of Nazi geno-cide against the Jews. Few people then or since have agreed.

On 16 October 1943 atrocity was enacted under the Pope's very windows: the deportation of the Jews of Rome began, from a depot ten minutes' walk from the Vatican. Pacelli's secretary of state, Cardinal Maglione, reminded the German ambassador in Rome, Ernst von Weizsacker, that the Pope had consistently avoided speaking against Germany, and declared that 'the Holy See should not be placed in a position where it is forced to protest'. Weizsacker promised to do what he could to stop the deportations, and Maglione left the matter in his hands. The deportations went ahead, the Vatican did not protest and Weizsacker told Berlin of his relief that the Pope had 'not allowed himself to be stampeded into making any demonstrative pronouncement against the removal of the Jews from Rome'.

The Pope's failure to condemn the deportation of the Roman Jews has come to focus the case against him. Little was said in his lifetime, but five years after Pacelli's death, Rolf Hochhuth's play, *The Deputy*, explained the Pope's silence in terms of anti-Semitism. Debate has raged ever since.

Why was he silent? It was certainly not a case of anti-Semitism. In the wake of the deportations on 16 October, colleges and other institutions in Vatican territory began hiding Roman Jews. Up to 5,000 were rescued, something that could not have happened without Pacelli's agreement. His defenders have pointed out that by and large the German forces respected Vatican territory, though they were aware that Jews were there. This immunity would certainly have vanished if the Pope had spoken out, and the hidden Jews would have been found and deported with the rest.

So was it concern for consequences? The Pope's housekeeper later claimed that Pius had in fact drafted a strong condemnation of the murder of European Jews in 1942, but burned it when the Nazis responded to the Dutch bishop's denunciation of the arrest of Jews by deporting all the baptised Jews as well. Protest was a luxury for which other people would die.

There was another possible reason. Pius knew about Nazi atrocities, but he was equally aware of Soviet atrocities, and he feared atheistic communism even more than Nazism. He believed, correctly, that if Germany were to be annihilated, nothing would stop Soviet advance into Europe. He repeatedly told allied leaders that he could denounce Nazi crimes only if he also denounced Soviet crimes.

Does all this amount to a defence? A papal condemnation of Nazi crimes might indeed have brought reprisals – for Catholics as well as for Jews – but it is clear that the German authorities *feared* a papal condemnation. It would have influenced public opinion and unsettled Catholics in Hitler's armies. And a declaration from the Pope might have alerted Europe, and Europe's Jews, to the real fate of those deported to 'work camps' in the east, and might have helped waken them to resistance.

The arguments from prudence are very weighty: Pacelli's commitment to papal impartiality was inherited from his great predecessor Benedict XV. And yet there still seems something lacking, something frozen, in Pacelli's response, even in his humanity. He was not the anti-Semitic monster of Hochhuth's play – he was silent in public even when Catholics were the victims – but in the face of one of the most terrible crimes in human history, impartial diplomacy and agonised calculation do not seem an adequate response from Christ's vicar on earth. When the helpless were being slaughtered, the most powerful voice in Christendom faltered, and fell silent.

9

JOHN XXIII

1958–1963

Few popes have been peasants. John XXIII, Angelo Roncalli, was one of the ten surviving children of a subsistence farmer from Bergamo; the family shared their farmhouse with their cattle. As was common in nineteenth-century Italy, Roncalli began studies for the priesthood at the age of twelve. Though interrupted by a spell in the ambulance corps during the First World War (when, to his subsequent embarrassment, he grew a walrus moustache), his career started well. For ten years he was secretary to the local bishop, before becoming professor of church history at the Bergamo seminary, and then he was recruited into one of the Vatican departments, fund-raising in Italy for mission work abroad.

For no very clear reason, things went wrong in the mid 1920s. Appointed professor in the Lateran University in Rome in 1924, he was relieved of his post after less than a year and given a mind-numbingly dull desk job. And in 1925, against his will, he was ordained bishop and sent as apostolic visitor to Bulgaria, where the Orthodox Church was deeply hostile to Catholicism. There had been no Vatican envoy for 600 years in what Rome clearly thought of as a godforsaken backwater, and the cardinal who despatched him admitted the job would be purgatory. Roncalli was promised a posting to Catholic Argentina if things went well but, in the event, he stayed in Bulgaria for ten years and was then moved to the equally obscure post of apostolic delegate to Greece and Turkey. The role of Vatican representative in an Orthodox or Islamic country might now be considered an important responsibility but in the 1930s it was ecclesiastical oblivion, a dumping ground for second-raters, and Roncalli knew he had been marginalised.

In his spiritual diary, he confided that the greatest trial of his life was not the incomprehension or hostility of the Orthodox or the Muslims (among whom he soon made friends) but the indifference and open contempt of his superiors in the Vatican. But he got on with the job, filling his spare hours with historical research and using his years in Istanbul to learn about and appreciate other ways of faith, and to build ties of humanity across religious divides.

With the outbreak of the Second World War, the deportation of Jews to concentration camps from German-occupied Greece began. Roncalli alerted the Vatican and mounted his own rescue operation, issuing thousands of diplomatic travel documents to help Jews escape. In 1945 Roncalli was transferred unexpectedly to the major post of nuncio to liberated France. But he was not to imagine, his Vatican boss informed him, that this promotion was any kind of accolade. General de Gaulle had demanded the removal of the wartime nuncio to France, the aristocratic Valerio Valeri, for collaborating with the Vichy regime. The demand angered Pius XII and he personally nominated Roncalli as replacement, possibly as a veiled rebuke to the haughty de Gaulle. The Pope is said to have remarked acidly, 'If they don't want an aristocrat, let them have a peasant.' Yet he must have considered Roncalli up to the demanding job.

De Gaulle was also insisting on the dismissal of more than thirty pro-Vichy bishops. It was a potential disaster: forced episcopal 'resignations' on this scale would brand the Church as collaborationist and un-French. Roncalli's warmth, simplicity of manner and obvious integrity defused the crisis, and only a handful of bishops were removed.

But Roncalli had more than simplicity to offer. His peasant shrewdness had been refined by an excellent education – he loved Latin literature and his conversation was laden with polyglot aphorisms and proverbs, ancient and modern. He was a hugely popular dinner guest, a notoriously 'heavy fork' with a liking for robust Lombard dishes – tripe à la Bergamo, polenta with game sauce, wild pig. His cheerful humanity and natural friendliness won people's trust, despite his conservative theology and his dutiful discharge of sometimes uncongenial Vatican policy.

In 1953 Pius XII made Roncalli a cardinal, at the advanced age of seventy-two, and named him Patriarch of Venice. He was overjoyed to be a pastoral bishop at last – Venice's parish priest, as he liked to call himself. Despite the efforts of the harassed officials managing his crammed diary, he never refused any visitor: 'Let them come in,' he would say, 'perhaps they want to go to confession.'

When Pius XII died in October 1958 it simply did not occur to Roncalli, now seventy-seven, that anyone would think him *papabile*, and he went to the Conclave with only an overnight bag. But after twenty years of Papa Pacelli's austere and some-times stifling autocracy, the cardinals were looking for something different. The obvious candidate was the brilliant Archbishop of Milan, Gianbattista Montini, but he was not yet a cardinal and so the Conclave looked for someone to keep the bed warm for a year or two. Roncalli, known as a 'holy old fogey' with no enemies, and because of his age unlikely to make drastic changes, seemed just the man. If there was laughter in heaven, no one at the Conclave heard it. Elected on the eleventh ballot, Roncalli took the name John XXIII, because his father was called John.

The pontificate of John XXIII transformed ecumenical relationships with the Churches of the Reformation. The visit of Queen Elizabeth II to the Vatican in 1961 followed hard on the heels of a visit the same year by the Archbishop of Canterbury, inaugurating closer relations with the Church of England.

John knew he did not have long, but it was clear from the start that he did not see himself as a mere stopgap. He was no revolutionary. He wanted 'aggiornamento', literally a bringing up to date, in all the Church's activity, but he had no master plan, and certainly no scheme for doctrinal or liturgical change; just humanisation, opening the windows. Aware of his own inexperience of the workings of the Vatican, he appointed as secretary of state his disapproving former boss in the diplomatic service, Cardinal Tardini, and he left in post many of the officials who had managed the Church in the sterile last years of Pius XII, notably

Pope John's Council, conducted in the full glare of global media attention, was arguably the most significant event in Christian history since the Reformation of the sixteenth century.

Cardinal Ottaviani, the fiercely reactionary head of the Vatican's most powerful department, the Holy Office. Their determined attempts to control him would be one of his greatest trials. He told the American Cardinal Cushing, 'I am in a bag here.'

But he astonished these battle-scarred old warriors within months of his election by announcing that he intended to summon a General Council. There had been talk of a Council under Pius XII, but what had been planned was a tame and largely mute assembly which would obediently nod through the Vatican agenda. John *had* no agenda, but he knew that the Church's response to modernity was in urgent need of reappraisal. He wanted an open Council whose priority was pastoral care for a needy world, not the maintenance of the barricades which the Vatican had been throwing up ever since the French Revolution.

As preparations for the Council got under way, he quietly began dismantling the state of siege. No pope for centuries had functioned as bishop of the diocese of Rome, leaving all such pastoral chores to a cardinal vicar, but John insisted on behaving like a real bishop, sallying out of the Vatican, often unannounced, to visit hospitals and prisons, acquainting himself with the Roman parishes. In place of the austere and carefully managed papal icon of Pius XII, Roncalli, tubby, smiling, big-eared and sometimes eccentrically dressed in the antique ermine papal bonnet he had revived, became familiar through a world press delighted and amazed to find there was a human being in the Vatican.

During the Cold War, the Vatican had forged a close relationship with the Italian Christian Democratic Party. John demanded that the Church distance itself from an unseemly conservative alliance that was corrupting for both sides. And,

Pius XII had seen world communism as the Church's greatest enemy, and he excommunicated any Italian who voted Communist: the dedication of Pasolini's Marxist portrait of Christ to Pope John XXIII was symptomatic of the many dramatic reversals initiated by his pontificate.

against appalled resistance within the Vatican, he also reversed Pius XII's Cold War policy in the international arena. Though he deplored communist ideology, he knew that many communists were sincere idealists fighting real injustice, and he thought it was time for a thaw towards the Eastern bloc. The gloomy denunciations of Pius XII's last years gave way to calls for dialogue between men of goodwill. The changed tone meant that during the Cuban Missile Crisis in October 1962 John's urgent peace appeal was taken seriously not only by the American president, the Catholic John F. Kennedy, but also by the

After the lofty austerity of Pius XII's public persona, John XXIII's spontaneous and pastoral approachability represented a new model for the papacy.

Soviet leader, Nikita Khrushchev, and it helped both sides to an honourable retreat. For the first time ever, *Pravda* printed part of a pope's Christmas message, and in March 1963 John warmly received Khrushchev's daughter and son-in-law in the Vatican. The Secretariat of State and the Holy Office worked frantically to prevent the visit. They imposed a blanket of silence on the Catholic press in a vain attempt to subvert the Pope's gesture. In 1964, the Italian communist film director, Pier Paolo Pasolini, dedicated his angry, Oscar-nominated film, *The Gospel According to St Matthew*, to John.

The Second Vatican Council opened in September 1962 and it too escaped the straitjacket that Vatican bureaucrats tried to impose on it. John wanted a Council for all Christians, creating a new Secretariat for Christian Unity. More than a hundred non-Catholic observers attended and played a major role in explaining the Council's work sympathetically to the wider Christian world. Two thousand Catholic bishops took part, and John entrusted the direction of policy to liberal bishops like Cardinal Montini of Milan, who would succeed him as Paul VI, and the Belgian Cardinal Suenens. In his opening address, the Pope, now a dying man, challenged the 'prophets of misfortune' who saw nothing in the world but 'betrayal and ruination', and called for a more open spirit in the Church, and for a willingness to think afresh about how the Christian message might be proclaimed today, 'for the substance of the ancient faith is one thing, and the way it is presented is another'. With this encouragement, the bishops rejected more than seventy draft documents prepared under Curial direction, and started from scratch, working to an agenda that they themselves had generated.

The Council met in the midst of the cultural and social upheavals of the 1960s and reflected them. It inaugurated a profound theological renewal whose implications have yet to be fully realised, triggered a drastic reappraisal of the relations between Church and society and initiated a reform of Catholic worship that would be characterised by drastic simplification and the virtual abandonment of the use of Latin. Some of this would have delighted John; some, like the loss of Latin, would have appalled him. He died in June 1963, three years before the Council completed its work.

It is hard to speak without sentiment of the greatness of a simply good man. But to anyone who lived through Pope John's quiet revolution, there can be no doubt about the nature or magnitude of his gift to the Church and to humanity. Catholicism before Papa Roncalli had many strengths, but it was overbearingly clerical, seeming both afraid and dismissive of the world around it, and though many of its people were warmly human, as an institution it existed in the deep freeze. In the hands of this good man, the ice began to melt.

10

JOHN PAUL II

1978–2005

W hen Karol Wojtyla was elected Pope John Paul II in 1978 at the age of fifty-eight, he seemed the best hope of reinvigorating a Church divided and adrift after a decade and a half of revolution. The Second Vatican Council had transformed Catholicism: the Latin liturgy had been simplified and translated into common speech; guitars and folk song replaced solemn plainchant; a centuries-old suspicion of secular modernity had given way to a sometimes naïve theological optimism; disdainful isolation from other Christians was replaced by enthusiastic ecumenism. But reform did not deliver the success many had hoped for. In the upheavals of the 1960s, Catholics shared the general collapse of confidence in venerable institutions and ideas. Thousands of priests, monks and nuns left to marry, recruitment halted, and there was widespread questioning of official doctrine and moral teaching. This came to a head in 1968 with unprecedented Catholic opposition to Pope Paul VI's encyclical, *Humanae Vitae*, which reiterated the Church's ban on artificial birth control. Some feared that concessions to reform had fatally compromised revealed truth and divine authority; others felt that the Council's call for more openness had been diverted and betrayed by a repressive papacy.

Wojtyla's dazzling talents and experience as a bishop in Cold War Poland seemed unique qualifications for resolving these tensions. He was a survivor of Nazi occupation, an athlete – apparently as much at home on the ski slope as in a pulpit – and he was a professional philosopher with two doctorates and a university chair behind him. He was a gifted linguist and a published poet and dramatist whose themes included sex as well as religion. At the Second Vatican Council he had championed religious freedom, calling especially for the abandonment of the Church's ancient and shameful ambivalence towards the Jews. As bishop he had been noted for his skill in outmanoeuvring the communist regime, but also for pastoral flair and a charismatic ministry to young intellectuals. A modern man, rooted in traditional values, free from compromising Vatican entanglements and surrounded by the heroic aura of the 'church of silence' behind the Iron Curtain, his election promised renewal after the stagnation and drift of Paul VI's last years. Here was a pope around whom Catholics could rally.

They got more than they bargained for. This 'man from a far country', the first non-Italian pope for 450 years, proved to be both an unashamed populist and a vigorous authoritarian. He would harness the resources of modernity – TV and the aeroplane – to re-establish an assertive papacy at the heart of Catholicism. In the wake of the Council many hoped that initiative would pass from Pope and Vatican to local bishops and their people. But Wojtyla believed that he should go and establish direct pastoral contact with Catholics everywhere, and he would become bishop to the whole world. He made more than a hundred international trips, in which he worked huge crowds with consummate skill, canonised more local saints than all his predecessors put together, and preached an uncompromising message of Christian fundamentals. Convinced that the churches of the West had been undermined by moral and doctrinal relativism, he called for a reassertion of Christian values and a halt to the liberalisms of the 1960s and '70s. Dispensations for priests and religious to marry dried up; religious orders were recalled to strict observance of their rules; hopes for a greater involvement

John Paul II returned to Poland the year after his election: despite government attempts to marginalise the visit, a third of the population turned out to see Wojtyla, and the Pope's presence provided the impetus for the foundation of the Solidarity union, and the movement for Polish liberation.

of bishops in policy-making were frustrated by growing centralisation – the English Cardinal Hume complained of being treated like an altar boy by Vatican officials. Promotions to the episcopate went increasingly to defenders of strict and sometimes blinkered orthodoxy, theologians were instructed to confine themselves to expounding official teachings, the intellectually adventurous were called to account. In 1994 he outlawed discussion of the ordination of women.

John Paul II was passionately committed to cooperation between the world's religions: his willingness to pray with non-Christians alarmed some of his theological advisers.

John Paul's moral teaching was directed above all against the 'culture of death' which he believed pervaded the modern world. We had created a culture in which birth control or abortion, rather than a just redistribution of the world's resources, were proposed as remedies for world hunger. He celebrated sexual love between married couples as an image of the self-giving life of God, but denounced the commodification of sex in the media. Inevitably, supporters and opponents alike focused on his sexual teaching. The American Bible Belt admired his absolute rejection of abortion, although they were less enthusiastic about his equally insistent opposition to war, to the possession of nuclear weapons, to the death penalty, and to the economic exploitation of the developing world by capitalism. Concerns for freedom and justice were abiding legacies of his Polish experience, and he used international visits to extract both from repressive regimes, from Chile to Cuba. However, he distrusted political theologies that seemed to him to dilute the Gospel with ideologies like Marxism, hence his discouragement of Liberation Theology.

John Paul's papacy, therefore, represented an attempt to steady the nerve of the Catholic Church by regrouping it round a strong papacy, and to evangelise a directionless world by the reassertion of strong Christian values. The policy proved divisive, increasingly alienating liberal opinion in Europe and North America, but delighting those who considered that the Second Vatican Council had inaugurated a 'silly season' whose aberrations would now be rolled back. Wojtyla defended the Council, but admired and promoted 'traditionalist' movements like *Opus Dei* which shared his robust confidence in ancient pieties and patterns of authority. In the longest papacy for a century, repressive clericalisms reasserted themselves in the Vatican and the wider church, aided by the Pope's evident lack of interest in management or institutional reform.

Yet he himself was never trapped in the sacristy, and his imagination and intuition often outran his concern for orthodoxy and order. Passionately convinced that we do not invent morality or truth, but find them in revelation and reason, he wanted to unite the world's religions in proclaiming the dignity of humanity and the goodness of God. Ignoring worried advice from Cardinal Ratzinger, head of the Church's Congregation for the Doctrine of the Faith (now Pope Benedict XVI), Papa Wojtyla inaugurated at Assisi a series of spectacular assemblies of world religious leaders, from Shinto priests to the Dalai Lama, and was the first pope to pray with 'non-Christians'. In the Jubilee year 2000, once more against the advice of his cautious aides, he presided at a series of public acts of repentance for the sins of the Catholic Church against human dignity. These culminated in a visit to Jerusalem during which the frail and trembling old man prayed at the Wailing Wall, posting there a letter of penitence for Christian atrocities, and a pledge of brotherhood with 'the people of the Covenant'. No pope in history has done more to heal the ancient wound of Christian anti-Semitism, just as no pope apart from himself had once played goalie in a Jewish football team.

Wojtyla was an untiring teacher, the most intelligent holder of his office for centuries. But his momentous pontificate is likely to be remembered above all for its Polish dimension. The Polish communist regime did not dare oppose his visit there in 1979, a year after his election. Attempts to disguise the scale of the immense and ecstatic crowds who turned out to greet him, by keeping TV cameras focused on Wojtyla alone, backfired when this consummate actor milked the opportunity, preaching a Gospel of human dignity and freedom subversive of the whole exercise. This and another triumphant visit there in 1983 shattered the apparent omnipotence of the communist state. His moral support was vital for the Solidarity movement (which he allegedly helped finance). It triggered a resurgence of national self-confidence that swept communism aside and accelerated the

dissolution of the Soviet bloc as a whole. Wojtyla didn't actually *cause* the collapse of communism, but in Poland, at least, he was the catalyst. No pope since the Middle Ages has had so direct and measurable an impact on world history. His lifelong dedication to freedom of conscience here bore its most spectacular fruit.

Wojtyla's last years were an agony, as his health failed and as traumatic revelations about sexual abuse by clergy in Europe and North America seemed to mock the Church's claim to speak for God. Vatican opposition to the use of condoms, never easy to explain to an uncomprehending secular world, was denounced as criminal irresponsibility in the face of the spread of Aids in Africa. The Pope's long decline from Parkinson's disease certainly damaged his Church – absolute monarchy works only so long as the monarch has the reins in his hands. Critics (and a few friends) called for his resignation, wondering why he clung to power. For John Paul, however, the lonely eminence of God's spokesman was not a power base but a service, a cross that had to be carried to the end. He understood and explained his infirmity as a final witness for the vulnerable, a manifesto against utilitarian measurements of human worth. As he struggled vainly to deliver his

Wojtyla's papacy was remarkable for a deliberate policy of rapprochement with Jews: in 1986 John Paul II was the first pope to visit the Roman Synagogue, and he was the first pope to recognise the State of Israel. During a visit to the Holy Land in March 2000 he prayed at the Wailing Wall in Jerusalem, and expressed his sorrow for Christian atrocities against the Jews.

last televised Easter message a week before his death in April 2005, he was visibly anguished by his dumbness, a titan in chains – and never more eloquent.

His death unleashed an extraordinary demonstration of mass grief, dwarfing that which attended the death of Princess Diana: four and a half million people flooded into Rome from all over the world and queued for eight, ten, thirteen hours to file past his body. His funeral, the largest media event in history, was given extended prime-time coverage by every TV and radio channel in the world. At his funeral Mass in St Peter's Square, two hundred world leaders and heads of state jostled for a place, including the Prince of Wales, who postponed his wedding to be there. Crowds of young people waved pictures of Wojtyla and chanted 'Santo subito' – 'canonise him *now*'.

Wojtyla's celebrity was an equivocal legacy to his Church, for who could match it? He was the greatest man to occupy the chair of Peter for centuries, and one of the greatest ever. His personal history recapitulated the tormented history of the twentieth century, and he brought to bear on that history an unflinching honesty of vision and an indomitable courage. He divided his Church, as he divided the secular world, but he was unquestionably the most remarkable man of his times.

FURTHER READING

GENERAL

Eamon Duffy, *Saints and Sinners: A History of the Popes* (New Haven and London, 2006). A one-volume survey of the whole of papal history.

J.N.D. Kelly, *The Oxford Dictionary of the Popes* (Oxford, 1986 and subsequent editions). Biographical entries with invaluable bibliographies for every pope and anti-pope up to John Paul II.

P. Levillain (ed.), *The Papacy: An Encyclopedia*, 3 vols (New York and London, 2002). More general coverage than Kelly, though the biographical entries are less comprehensive.

ST PETER

Marcus Bockmuehl, 'Peter's Death in Rome? Back to front and upside down', *Scottish Journal of Theology*, 60/1 (2007), pp. 1–23, surveys the controversies and defends the tradition of Peter's death in Rome.

Oscar Cullmann, *Peter, Disciple, Apostle, Martyr: A Historical and Theological Study* (Norwich, 1962).

E. Kirschbaum, *The Tombs of St Peter and St Paul* (London, 1959).

D.W. O'Connor, *Peter in Rome: The Literary, Liturgical, and Archeological Evidence* (New York, 1969).

LEO THE GREAT

There is sadly little modern writing in English on Leo. The standard life in English is still T.G. Jalland, *The Life and Times of St Leo the Great* (London, 1941). Walter Ullmann, 'Leo I and the theme of Papal Primacy', *Journal of Theological Studies*, XI/1 (1960), pp. 25–51, is the most important study of Leo's teaching on the papacy.

GREGORY THE GREAT

The best recent biography is Jeffrey Richards, *Consul of God* (London, 1980). Robert Markus, *Gregory the Great and His World* (Cambridge, 1997) locates Gregory in late antiquity. For her thought, see Carole E. Straw, *Gregory the Great: Perfection in Imperfection* (Berkeley, 1988). See also the collection of essays edited by John Cavadini, *Gregory the Great: A Symposium* (Notre Dame, IN, 1995).

INNOCENT III

The best biographical study is Helene Tillmann, *Pope Innocent III* (Amsterdam, 1980), and there is a useful overview by Jane Sayers, *Innocent III: Leader of Europe, 1198–1216* (London, 1988). A fascinating anonymous contemporary account of Innocent has been edited and translated by James L. Powell as *The Deeds of Pope Innocent III* (Washington, DC, 2004).

PAUL III

There is no good modern biography of Paul III, and none at all in English. The relevant volume of Ludwig Pastor, *History of the Popes* (London, 1891–1953) is the best place to start. An entertaining account of the Farnese family is by G.R. Solari (trans. F. Tuten and S. Morini), *The House of Farnese: A Portrait of a Great Family of the Renaissance* (New York, 1968). There is much on Paul III and his pontificate in the first two volumes of H. Jedin (trans.), *History of the Council of Trent* (London, 1957 and 1961). The best study of the reforming circle promoted by Paul III is Dermot Fenlon, *Heresy and Obedience in Tridentine Italy: Cardinal Pole and the Counter Reformation* (Cambridge, 1972).

PIO NONO

The best biography of Pio Nono, G. Martina, *Pio IX*, 3 vols (Rome, 1967–90), has still not been translated into English. E.E.Y. Hales, *Pio Nono* (London, 1954) is elderly but worth reading, while Frank Coppa's *Pope Pius IX: Crusader in a Secular Age* (Boston, 1979) is drier but informative. Owen Chadwick's entertaining *A History of the Popes, 1830–1914* (Oxford, 1998) is probably the most balanced survey.

PIUS XII

The literature on Pius XII is an ever-expanding minefield. The most recent biography, P. Chenaux, *Pie XII: Diplomate et Pasteur* (Paris, 2003) has not been translated. John Cornwell, *Hitler's Pope: The Secret History of Pius XII* (London, 1999) is very readable but, as the title suggests, is the case for the prosecution. On the vexed issue of the 'silence' of Pius XII, two books make a good point of entry: Owen Chadwick, *Britain and the Vatican during the Second World War* (Cambridge, 1986) and José M. Sanchez, *Pius XII and the Holocaust: Understanding the Controversy* (Washington, DC, 2002).

JOHN XXIII

Peter Hebblethwaite, *John XXIII: Pope of the Council* (London, 1984; rev. Margaret Hebblethwaite, 2000) remains the best biography. Papa Roncalli's journals were edited as Pope John XXIII, *Journal of a Soul*, trans. Dorothy White (London, 1965).

For the debate about the history of John's Council, see John W. O'Malley, *What Happened at Vatican II* (Cambridge, MA, 2008).

JOHN PAUL II

A full and highly laudatory biography in English is George Weigel, *Witness to Hope: The Biography of Pope John Paul II*, rev. edn (New York, 2005). For a briefer but equally laudatory account, see Garry O'Connor, *Universal Father: A Life of John Paul II* (London, 2006). Edward Stourton, *John Paul II: Man of History* (London, 2006) is more astringent. For his thought, see Avery Dulles, *The Splendor of Faith: The Theological Vision of Pope John Paul II* (New York, 1999).

INDEX

Index created by Meg Davies
(Fellow of the Society of Indexers)